How to Lead a Healthy Small Group

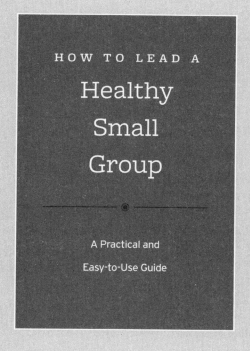

HOW TO LEAD A

# Healthy
# Small
# Group

A Practical and

Easy-to-Use Guide

# Kevin Mills
## THOM S. RAINER, SERIES EDITOR

TYNDALE
MOMENTUM®

*A Tyndale nonfiction imprint*

Visit Tyndale online at tyndale.com.

Visit Tyndale Momentum online at tyndalemomentum.com.

*Tyndale*, Tyndale's quill logo, *Tyndale Momentum*, and the Tyndale Momentum logo are registered trademarks of Tyndale House Ministries. Tyndale Momentum is a nonfiction imprint of Tyndale House Publishers, Carol Stream, Illinois.

*How to Lead a Healthy Small Group: A Practical and Easy-to-Use Guide*

Designed by Ron C. Kaufmann

All Scripture quotations are taken from the Holy Bible, *New International Version,*® *NIV.*® Copyright © 1973, 1978, 1984, 2011 by Biblica, Inc.® Used by permission. All rights reserved worldwide.

For information about special discounts for bulk purchases, please contact Tyndale House Publishers at csresponse@tyndale.com, or call 1-855-277-9400.

**Library of Congress Cataloging-in-Publication Data**

A catalog record for this book is available from the Library of Congress.

ISBN 978-1-4964-6204-6

Printed in the United States of America

| 28 | 27 | 26 | 25 | 24 | 23 | 22 |
|----|----|----|----|----|----|----|
| 7  | 6  | 5  | 4  | 3  | 2  | 1  |

# Contents

# Introduction

"WHAT'S YOUR FAVORITE BOOK OF THE BIBLE?"

I've been asked this question numerous times—and not just because I'm a pastor. The question has been posed in various group settings as an icebreaker or discussion starter. It's always interesting to hear how people answer and the reasons they give for why a particular book of the Bible ranks at the top of their list.

I don't know that I've ever heard anyone ask, "What's your *least* favorite book of the Bible?" Not many Christ followers would want to answer that one. Any response sounds like a criticism of God's Word. It's like asking, "What's your least favorite thing about your spouse?"

*"I'll plead the Fifth, thank you."*

But I'm going to go out on a limb here and answer the question about my least favorite book of the Bible.

*Ecclesiastes.*

Without a doubt.

I'm convinced that Solomon was clinically depressed when he wrote Ecclesiastes. Though he had wealth, power, and access to every pleasure and creature comfort of life, he was absolutely miserable. Everything was pointless to him. His life had no purpose. He found himself swimming in a deep sea of meaninglessness.

If you're depressed, don't read Ecclesiastes. I can sum it up for you: Solomon examines virtually every aspect of life and concludes that nothing really matters. Whether it's work, money, pleasure, or achievements, at the end of the day, they're all just pointless pursuits. According to Solomon, there isn't anything in our short lives that's actually worth our time and energy.

Well, except for one: *relationships*.

In one of the few bright spots in the book, Solomon recognizes the great value of friendships:

Two are better than one,
    because they have a good return for their labor. . . .
Though one may be overpowered,
    two can defend themselves.
A cord of three strands is not quickly broken.
ECCLESIASTES 4:9, 12

In this passage, Solomon reminds us that we are designed to live in community with others. Relationships are not optional. According to the wisest man (other than Jesus) who ever lived, friendships are the one commodity truly worth pursuing.

When we step back from Ecclesiastes and look at the Bible as a whole, we find an oft-repeated theme: *Love God and love others*. In other words, the two things that matter most in life are a relationship with God and relationships with other people. Everything else falls way down the list.

Healthy churches emphasize both of these pursuits, and they do it most effectively through small groups. Arguably, this is the most important ministry in your church. Organizing, promoting, and supporting small groups create the necessary environment for teaching people how to love God and love one another. Any church with a healthy small group structure and committed small group leaders will be a healthy, growing church. Conversely, any church without healthy small groups is undoubtedly an unhealthy church.

This is where *you* come in. Someone has observed God's hand on your life. They've noticed your heart for the Lord and your love for others. They've recognized your gifts in teaching and leading others. And now they've asked you to consider leading a small group in your church. Perhaps they're hoping you and your spouse will together lead a couples group. Or you've been asked to lead a group of singles, men, or women.

After praying about the matter, you said *yes*. You want to make a difference for God's Kingdom. Your greatest joy is seeing God change people's lives. You're willing to do whatever it takes to assist in the ministry of your church.

However, despite everything, you feel ill-equipped to lead a group. Like many Christians, your desire to minister exceeds your knowledge of how to do so. Yet you want to be better prepared to do the work God has for you.

My hope is that this book will add several useful items to your ministry tool belt—combining scriptural guidelines with practical ideas for leading your small group more effectively. By God's grace, and through your attention to what his Word teaches, you can shepherd your group well. Healthy, focused groups will change lives and change your church.

If you feel you're not qualified, you're exactly right. Apart from God himself, nobody's up to the task. However, when you realize you're not enough, you'll find that God is more than enough. He will surely reward your faithfulness.

—*Kevin Mills*

1

# A Holy Calling

*Your Role as a Small Group Leader*

WHEN I FIRST MET Zach and Ashley, they were recent college graduates. Both had grown up going to church most Sundays. Zach's family lived in a rural community and attended a small country church. Ashley's family lived in a suburb and were members of a traditional, mainline-denomination church. But by the time they met, during their sophomore year in college, neither one was going to church other than for the obligatory Easter and Christmas services with their families. Though both would say they were Christians, their faith made only a minimal difference in their lives.

They dated throughout college, married after graduation, and accepted jobs in our suburban community. After purchasing their first home, they began to settle into their new life together.

My small group leader at the time lived across the street from

5

Zach and Ashley. One evening, he and his wife, with a pound cake in hand, walked over to greet their new neighbors. Zach and Ashley knew virtually no one in our community and were excited to meet another couple. They stood in the front doorway and talked for more than an hour. As they parted ways, my small group leader said to Zach and Ashley, "You know, there's a group that meets at our house on Thursday nights for a Bible study. We'd love to have you join us. Just come on over at seven o'clock if you're interested."

The previous year had been such a whirlwind of activity—getting engaged, planning for and having the wedding, moving to a new community, and starting new jobs—that Zach and Ashley hadn't discussed church or much of anything else about their spiritual lives. However, they were looking for friendships, and this was their first opportunity to meet some new people.

The next Thursday, they nervously walked across the street. I first met them standing in the kitchen of my small group leader's home. They didn't ask, and I didn't volunteer that I was a pastor. At no point did anyone in our small group announce that we all attended the same church. We read from the Bible, we discussed the passage, and we prayed for one another. Zach and Ashley left at the end of the night, and I privately wondered if they'd return.

But they were back the following week. And the week after that.

On their fourth consecutive week attending the Bible study, Zach suddenly interrupted the group and said, "Hey, I've got a question. Do all of you go to the same church?"

We all nodded, not realizing that Zach and Ashley hadn't known that.

Zach looked at Ashley, grabbed her hand, and turned back to the group.

"Ashley and I want you guys to know what a difference this Bible study has made in our lives. Since we've been coming here on Thursday nights, we're having discussions we've never had before. We're reconnecting with God and talking about how we want our marriage to look and how we want to raise our family. This has had a huge impact us. If you all go to the same church, we want to come on Sunday. Just tell us what time it starts and how to get there."

Zach and Ashley have since moved on to a community in another part of our state. Recently, when they came through town on their way to a vacation destination, my wife and I had dinner with them. They talked about their jobs and their new home, but mostly they talked about their church. They've plugged into a small group. They are serving in the congregation. They are faithful in their giving and in their attendance.

They now have a four-year-old son. When they put him to bed at night, they read to him from a children's Bible. He attends Sunday school and participates in Vacation Bible School and other activities offered by the church. Zach and Ashley are doing everything they can to raise their son in a way that will incline his heart toward the Lord.

Zach's and Ashley's lives were changed through the ministry of a local church small group, and that impact is now being felt in the next generation as well. There will likely come a day when their son falls in love, gets married, and has a family of his own. My prayer is that he will instruct his children in the same principles he's now being taught.

And it all started when a small group leader invited them to a Bible study.

Your role as a small group leader is a holy calling. The Lord

7

will use it to change lives, marriages, and families—potentially for generations to come.

According to Thom Rainer, who for nearly forty years has been committed to the growth and health of the local church and its leaders, individuals are five times more likely to assimilate into the life of a church if they are involved in a group, instead of attending worship only.[1] A healthy, positive group experience is the key to connecting people with a church and helping them continue to grow in their faith.

In the last chapter of Matthew, we read the following instructions from Jesus to his followers:

> Go and make disciples of all nations, baptizing them in the name of the Father and of the Son and of the Holy Spirit, and teaching them to obey everything I have commanded you. And surely I am with you always, to the very end of the age.
>
> MATTHEW 28:19-20

These are the church's marching orders: *Go and make disciples.* This is our mission.

Notice that Jesus didn't say, "Go and make converts." Neither did he say, "Go and make church members," nor, "Go and make good, upstanding citizens." He said, "Go and make *disciples.*"

In other words, go and make people whose lives are continually shaped by the gospel; who follow Christ daily—not perfectly, but faithfully; whose lives will change the culture around them; who will leave a legacy of faith to their families, friends, communities, and generations to come.

---

[1] Thom S. Rainer, "What Does Your Church's Group Name Communicate?," *Church Answers* (blog), October 7, 2015, https://churchanswers.com/blog/what-does-your-churchs-group-name-communicate/.

I don't think I can overstate the importance and the significance of your calling as a small group leader. Eternity is on the line. The future of the church is at stake. The spiritual war in your community will be won or lost on the front lines of small group ministry. Your role as a leader is holy, invaluable, and essential in your local church and the church at large.

When I arrived at my current ministry in 2007, we had only a handful of small groups in our church. The congregation had endured a troubled season, and the difficulties had seeped into the small group meetings. Soon, discussions centered far more on events happening in the church than on the evening's biblical text or study. Over the course of the previous year, half the members and regular attenders had left the church, and most of the small groups simply dissolved. By the time I arrived, only a few groups still met, and even those had dwindled in their attendance. Instead of "small groups," we could have called them "tiny groups."

It was tough.

There were no stories of life change. There were no baptisms. The ministry of the church was frozen. I realized quickly that our church was like an ocean diver whose oxygen line had been severed. If we didn't repair this lifeline soon, we simply weren't going to make it.

I hired a small groups pastor, and we rolled up our sleeves and went to work. We looked at our numbers and assessed the situation. We reviewed the names of past leaders and small group members. For a while, we faced the challenge of ascertaining who was in and who was out. We made countless phone calls. We had untold lunch and coffee meetings. Those initial months took a lot of boots-on-the-ground work.

I met personally with every leader who remained at the church. I talked about the importance of small groups to the purpose and mission of the church. I shared honestly about our lack of leaders and the need to revitalize our small group ministry. I asked if they were willing to join me in leading a small group.

Several told me they couldn't. They either were not in a healthy place spiritually, or they held lingering bitterness in their hearts. They knew they wouldn't be able to lead a small group effectively.

Others took the opportunity to let me know they had decided to leave the church. Those were hard conversations.

However, a number agreed to serve and help us reignite our small group ministry. They worked with us to recruit members. We equipped them with resources and did our best to train and retrain leaders. After some time, the heart of our small group ministry began beating again. People met and prayed, studied the Bible, encouraged one another, cared for one another, and held one another accountable. They grew in their faith.

You can probably guess what happened next. We began to grow as a church—both spiritually and numerically. With a healthy (or at least *healthier*) small group ministry, the other components of the church began to operate more effectively. Worship was more powerful. Giving increased. More people came to outreach events. It was easier to recruit volunteers.

Why did all this happen? Because we were once again *making disciples*.

At the risk of sounding like a broken record, I'm going to say it again: Your role as a small group leader is critical in the church. It is a holy calling. Your pastor and other leaders greatly appreciate your willingness to step up. Your ministry is vital to the health of your local church and to the spread of the gospel around the world.

Thank you for serving in this way.

**2**

# The Right Model

*Defining a Healthy Small Group*

I RECENTLY WENT to my family doctor for my annual physical. It's an appointment I always dread. It's not that I dislike my doctor; in fact, I think we could probably be good friends outside of our doctor/patient relationship. He's funny, interesting, and genuinely concerned about my health. But, ay, there's the rub. At my appointment, he opens his fancy laptop and shares with me all the characteristics of a healthy individual. Then he compares my numbers with "healthy ranges" defined by the AMA, CDC, WebMD, or some other such alphabet organization.

It's all a numbers game. My bad cholesterol is too high. My good cholesterol needs to be higher. My blood pressure should be lower. My BMI could come down a few points as well.

The blood work report has lots of codes and numbers that can be quite confusing; however, they all indicate something important

11

about my physical health. If my numbers are in a healthy range, the doctor puts a check mark in the adjacent box. If they're not in a healthy range, I get a phone call and my doctor clearly outlines where I need to change my ways and the goals I need to set. Although I'm not particularly fond of his obsession with numbers, I'm thankful for the conversation because he shows me the right path to achieve optimal physical health.

You can evaluate small groups in a similar way. No, you won't have to give any blood, but certain indicators will tell you whether a small group is healthy or unhealthy.

Sadly, in many churches the members have never been exposed to a healthy small group model. And like someone growing up in a dysfunctional family, who assumes that every family acts like theirs, members of a dysfunctional small group can start to believe it's normal for people to speak harshly to one another, or for leaders to pit group members against each other in passive-aggressive conflict.

People who have never experienced a healthy small group will assume that unhealthy is normal; that dysfunctional is just the way it is; and that a group committed to life change and faith building is an aberration.

## Five Types of Unhealthy Small Groups

Over the years, I've observed five types of unhealthy small groups.

### 1. Therapeutic groups

These are groups whose primary goal is for the members to provide emotional support for one another. If they read a passage of Scripture, the members will immediately steer the conversation away from the meaning of the text and onto their own personal issues.

*I'm mad at my roommate.*

*My boss is a jerk.*

*My dog has fleas. Can we spend just a little more time talking about how awful it is to live with fleas?*

Therapeutic groups thrive on bad news. Discussions about good things the Lord is doing are cut short. Group members enjoy wallowing in the mud of negative emotions; they're not really happy unless they're miserable.

## 2. Political groups

Members of this type of group are able to take virtually any Bible passage and explain how it relates to our current political climate. They will spend the vast majority of their time talking about the upcoming election, or the previous election, or the liberal bias of the media, or the whacky conservatives, or whatever current buzz is on the news cycle. Though they would never admit it, they believe the salvation of our country is based on the election of a certain political party and getting specific types of justices appointed to the US Supreme Court.

These members aren't really interested in the gospel changing lives unless the gospel also changes the political views of those individuals. They love it when their pastor preaches a message addressing a social ill in our nation. That is, unless they disagree with the pastor's stance on the issue. Then the small group time is used to discuss the poor pastor's misguided views.

## 3. Social groups

The members of this type of group spend the majority of their time fellowshipping. They will talk about the football games they watched the day before, or where they are planning to go on vacation, or how their kids and grandkids are doing. If they've allotted an hour for their meeting, they will spend forty-five minutes talking, five minutes reading and discussing the Bible passage, and nine minutes taking prayer requests before someone offers a one-minute closing prayer. They love to eat together, golf together, shop together, or grab coffee and just talk. The small group is essentially their friend group.

The members of these groups aren't averse to discussing the gospel as long as they do so quickly. They are happy to hear good news about what the Lord is doing in the lives of group members; however, they get very uncomfortable when things get too spiritual. As they see it, the point of a small group is just to be close to one another. Too much talk about Jesus can be divisive and ruin the fellowship.

## 4. Gripe groups

This is the grumpy old men group—although the members might very well be young and/or female. These groups love to talk about their ailments, or problems in the church, or everything that's wrong with the world. A black cloud hangs over these groups, and it's the negativity that binds members together.

These group members tend to stay together for a long time simply because no other group wants them. They aren't interested in hearing about great things the Lord is doing in the church because that doesn't fit their narrative. For them, the sky is falling or is about to fall. They love drama—especially drama in the church. A nugget of gossip about the pastor is a beautiful thing and will be admired for an entire meeting. Their motto is, "If you don't have anything nice to say about someone, then come and stand next to me. I'll be happy to listen."

## 5. Silent groups

This type of group is dominated by a teacher who sees it as his or her mission to download as much information as possible to the group. Meetings consist of long lectures, and no one dares to ask any questions. The members are happy because they don't have to talk, and the leader is happy because he or she gets to do all the talking. Members are satisfied to hear about the gospel, politics, gossip, or anything else the teacher wants to bring up. They aren't expected to open up and share anything about themselves or their relationship with God. They are content to sit with their Bibles open in their laps and allow the leader to do all the heavy lifting.

Why are these five groups unhealthy? Because they are not meeting the purposes of a small group.

Notice what Acts 2 says about the early church:

They devoted themselves to the apostles' teaching and
to fellowship, to the breaking of bread and to prayer.
Everyone was filled with awe at the many wonders and
signs performed by the apostles. All the believers were
together and had everything in common. They sold
property and possessions to give to anyone who had need.
Every day they continued to meet together in the temple
courts. They broke bread in their homes and ate together
with glad and sincere hearts, praising God and enjoying
the favor of all the people. And the Lord added to their
number daily those who were being saved.

ACTS 2:42-47

The book of Acts is more than just a historical account of the early church; we also find insights there about how we as individuals and churches should live out our faith. In this passage, Luke gives a snapshot of life among the first disciples. Really, it's more like a collage composed of several different pictures. In one photo, we see believers gathered in the Temple courts, listening to the apostles teach the same truths that Jesus taught. Another image shows a man selling a piece of property so that the money might be used to help others in the church. There's a picture of a crowd looking on in amazement as one of the apostles miraculously heals a man who had been disabled since birth.

Additionally, there is a photo of a small group gathering in someone's home. They are seated on the floor around a low table full of food. They are laughing, eating, and enjoying one another's company.

## Three Traits of Healthy Small Groups

Acts 2:42-47 gives us guidance on the ideal characteristics of a small group.

### 1. Healthy small groups are centered on God's Word

Notice how members of the early church devoted themselves to the teachings of the apostles. Why did they commit their time to listening to these men in particular? Because the apostles weren't sharing their own thoughts and feelings. They repeated what Jesus taught them. They relayed the stories we now read in the four Gospels. They retold the parables they had heard from Jesus. They gave the same instructions, commands, and encouragements that Jesus gave them. What the apostles taught was so much more than simply their opinions; they were words of truth from the very one who said, "I am the way and the truth and the life" (John 14:6).

Healthy small groups must have a similar focus. Spending time talking about college football, children, the local news, national news, or the weather is fine. Discussing our feelings on an issue is perfectly acceptable. Sharing something an author wrote on a certain topic is quite normal. However, the central focus of the group should be studying the Word of God.

Why is this so important? Because we are all flawed human beings. As the leader, you have much to offer, but like the rest of us, you're not perfect. If the focus of your small group study is your own thoughts and opinions, or those of your group members, or the writings of some author, group members could be led astray.

However, the Word of God is perfect, infallible, and time-tested. Studying the teachings of Jesus, the apostles, and the Old Testament saints will always lead the members of your group in the right direction.

Moreover, true life change occurs when we discover the wonderful truths contained in God's Word. Books and videos can be good and helpful—especially when they focus on or expound upon God's Word. But no author or speaker, no matter how gifted, has the power with their own words to do what the Bible will do in our hearts.

Notice what the author of Hebrews writes about this issue:

The word of God is alive and active. Sharper than any double-edged sword, it penetrates even to dividing soul and spirit, joints and marrow; it judges the thoughts and attitudes of the heart.

HEBREWS 4:12

The ultimate goal for your members is that their faith in God will grow through their participation in your group. True life change comes from studying God's Word.

In our church, we offer a variety of books and videos as resources for our small group leaders. There are studies on marriage, parenting, understanding the will of God, how to share one's faith, and a number of other topics. Many in our church have benefited greatly as a result of their small group using one or more of these resources. However, I always encourage our small groups to take at least some time to read through and study a book of the Bible together. I advise you to do the same.

Don't feel the need to spend hours reading commentaries or parsing Greek verbs to prepare for your meeting. There is great value in simply reading through the text and posing questions to the members of your group about the meaning of what you've read.

Like many others, my small group was forced to meet via Zoom during the early days of the COVID-19 pandemic. Though videoconferencing is now widely used by most people in the business world, this was the first time our small group met using this format. Our leader wisely decided to walk through the book of Ephesians during those weeks. Members took turns reading a portion of the passage and answering a few questions our group leader prepared. It proved to be one of our best studies. Hardly anyone missed a meeting. In the midst of a worldwide pandemic, economic uncertainty, and social isolation, we found it quite refreshing to be reminded of God's "incomparably great power for us who believe" (Ephesians 1:19), that "he himself is our peace" (Ephesians 2:14), and that he "is able to do immeasurably more than all we ask or imagine, according to his power that is at work within us" (Ephesians 3:20). Through that study, God's Word fed my soul, something I sorely needed during those strange times.

Your small group will be healthier if you focus on the Bible.

### 2. Healthy small groups care for one another well

Acts 2 gives us various pictures of life in the early church. We could easily add several more based on other descriptions in the New Testament—for example, two believers in a home praying together; a couple of deacons taking food to an elderly widow; individuals from Stephen's small group sitting with his widow, offering her emotional support, cleaning her home, and raising money to provide for her and her children. Acts and the remainder of the New Testament clearly show us how the early church members lived in tightly knit communities, experiencing life together in many different ways.

There are approximately forty "one another" commands in the New Testament. These are instructions about how we are to operate in the context of a faith community. Notice just a few of these verses describing how your small group should relate to one another:

- *Love* one another (John 13:34).
- *Be devoted* to one another in love (Romans 12:10).
- *Live in harmony* with one another (Romans 12:16).
- *Accept* one another (Romans 15:7).
- *Encourage* one another (2 Corinthians 13:11).
- *Serve* one another *humbly in love* (Galatians 5:13).
- *Forgive* one another (Colossians 3:13).

This list is only a sampling of what the Bible teaches about the proper functioning of the body of Christ. We are to love and care for each other in ways that promote our fellow members' best interests. This means being there for others when they are hurting or offering support when they are facing a personal crisis. It means challenging others to grow in their faith by encouraging them to attend meetings or gently confronting them about a sin issue. In all our interactions, we want to do everything we can to nudge each other closer to Christ.

The great wisdom of King Solomon sums up the purpose of a healthy small group: "As iron sharpens iron, so one person sharpens another" (Proverbs 27:17). Your small group is designed to be a place where members sharpen each other's faith. As you love, pray for, challenge, encourage, and serve one another well, your small group will become healthier.

### 3. Healthy small groups reach out and multiply

Your goal is to expand your membership, either by adding members to your group or by multiplying and starting new groups. A stagnant, never-changing, inwardly focused small group is inherently unhealthy.

A number of years ago, my wife and I began serving as foster parents. Like many families who step into this role, we eventually adopted two children who had been placed in our home. Along with our biological son and daughter, we now had four children, all seven years old and younger. To say the least, it was overwhelming. As Katie and I discussed the future and the question of whether we should continue as foster parents now that we had adopted these two, she heard me continually repeat the same phrase: "*Four and no more.*" We had zero margin left in our lives, and I felt it would be unwise to add any more children through fostering, adoption, or biological means. Whenever Katie broached the topic, she would see the look in my eyes and simply say, "I know, I know. Four and no more."

Though that was the right approach for our family when it came to having children, "four and no more" is not a healthy model for a small group. Neither is "six and no more" or "twelve and no more." Small groups must have a missional mindset, ready to be used by the Lord to reach people with the gospel. If your small group ministry is growing to such a degree that more groups are needed, that is an outcome to celebrate, not stifle.

Go back to the collection of snapshots of the early church found in Acts 2:42-47. Of all the pictures in that paragraph, my favorite is found in the last two sentences: "They broke bread in their homes and ate together with glad and sincere hearts, praising God and enjoying the favor of all the people. And the Lord added to their number daily those who were being saved" (vv. 46-47). I love this example of gathering in homes, sharing meals with one another, and worshiping together. That's a blueprint for a thriving small group ministry. And when the outside world witnessed this, they desperately wanted to become part of the fellowship.

One could argue that it was the small group ministry of the early church that drove the exponential growth. Outsiders took note of the church's unique gatherings and longed to experience that kind of community. The appeal of these small groups caused others to ask questions, opening the door for the gospel to be shared.

The result?

*The Lord added daily to their numbers.*

Healthy small groups may be the best and most effective evangelism tool for your church. Every person on the planet needs healthy, dynamic relationships.

Yes, we all have an innate need for God (Ecclesiastes 3:11). But many in our world today have worked to suppress this deep-seated desire of the human heart (Romans 1:18). On the other hand, very few have rebelled against the equally God-given longing we have for community. Regardless of their beliefs about God, sin, and salvation, the vast majority of people in the world desperately need and eagerly desire close connections with others. Therefore, a healthy, thriving small group ministry will *attract* the lost and the lonely to your church and to the gospel. Because people naturally yearn for community, a local church with healthy small groups will draw outsiders into the fellowship.

Moreover, the Bible is clear that the Holy Spirit is very much involved in our mandate to go and make disciples. If healthy small groups are integral to this process, where do you think the Holy Spirit will lead lost people? To a church with unhealthy small groups, or to a church with healthy small groups, where individuals will actually grow in their faith?

The answer is clear. This is why healthy, growing churches tend to experience continual growth while plateaued and declining churches struggle to reach people. Growth begets growth, and healthy small groups are the impetus for this to happen in your church. A church filled with healthy small groups will be an unstoppable force in spreading the gospel. Life-on-life gospel conversations, in the context of a small group environment, will produce disciples far more effectively than evangelistic crusades or door-to-door witnessing.

God isn't expecting your group to be perfect. However, you should certainly strive to be healthy. Following the early church's model is the best place to start.

# 3

# The Bigger Picture

*Operating within the Ministry of the Church*

"I'M FRUSTRATED AND READY TO QUIT."

I had been talking on the phone for nearly an hour with a pastor I knew when he made this statement. I distinctly remember him telling me about all the troubles in his church. He couldn't point to any one issue, but things were just not going well. I had listened to a handful of his sermons, and he was clearly a good preacher and teacher of God's Word. His church had an attractive campus, offered solid programming for children and students, and supported local and international mission efforts. Most outsiders would have described it as an active, healthy church.

Except it wasn't. The church had been plateaued for a decade. Very few families from the community were visiting, and even fewer joined the church.

The stagnation had begun under the previous pastor, who

had essentially operated on cruise control for the last several years of his ministry. Moreover, he and his wife had remained in the church after he retired, and his continuing presence—and the occasional comments he made about his successor—didn't help the new pastor's ministry. A malaise had settled over the congregation. Complaints and grumblings dominated many of their conversations.

According to the pastor, the airing of grievances happened chiefly in small group meetings. Instead of studying the Bible and praying together, members spent the majority of their time dissecting the pastor's latest decisions. Or complaining about a ministry. Or whining about the lack of growth in the church. The pastor received regular reports from small group leaders on the discontentment within their ranks. Everywhere he turned, it seemed, someone was whining, muttering, and moaning about the state of the church. The ministry couldn't move forward with gossip and complaints dominating every discussion.

Years ago, another pastor shared with me about a Sunday school class in his church that had gone rogue. The leader was incredibly gifted, both organizationally and as a teacher. In a church of five or six hundred, the class routinely had more than one hundred in attendance each Sunday. The class met in the church's fellowship hall because there was no classroom large enough to accommodate them. This group had essentially become their own church, with the teacher serving as their de facto pastor. Although still part of the congregation, they operated as a separate entity from the rest of the church.

Sadly, I could tell you many other stories about church conflict that first took root in the small group ministry. Instead of strengthening the congregation, these meetings do more harm than good. Though the group members may be unified, they are a source of division in the church. Their meetings and their members become a hindrance to the overall ministry.

Of course, this is not unique to the twenty-first century American church. One of the earliest accounts of divisive small groups is found in Paul's first letter to the church in Corinth, where several groups had gone off the rails. Their meetings caused divisions within the congregation. Paul wrote about this issue to the entire fellowship in Corinth, but specifically named these small groups:

> What I mean is this: One of you says, "I follow Paul"; another, "I follow Apollos"; another, "I follow Cephas"; still another, "I follow Christ."
>
> I CORINTHIANS 1:12

The small group meetings in Corinth had turned into discussions about their favorite pastor. Some favored Paul, the founder of the church. Others were fans of Apollos, the second pastor and—by all accounts—an incredibly gifted teacher. Some members connected with Peter, who had most likely preached in Corinth and impressed many with his stories of walking with Jesus. Other members saw themselves as super-spiritual and were unwilling to follow any human leader. "We answer only to Jesus," they smugly proclaimed.

It was a mess. These groups created schisms in the church. Their meetings were so destructive that Paul spent roughly a quarter of his letter addressing the need for unity. The divisions hamstrung the ministry. Paul desperately wanted the congregation to unify.

Why is church unity so important? Because there is tremendous lostness in your community. Your church has an opportunity to depopulate hell, but it cannot do this effectively without unity among the membership. You are a catalyst for setting the right tone in your group. Your leadership in this area will bolster the church's overall health and the effectiveness of the ministry. Therefore, your efforts to foster unity are critical to reaching your community with the gospel.

How can you effectively lead your small group in this way?

## Three Biblical Guidelines for Small Group Leaders

Consider these three biblical guidelines for small group leaders:

### 1. Operate under the authority of church leadership

Reread what Acts 2:42 says about how the early church functioned:

> They devoted themselves to the apostles' teaching and to fellowship, to the breaking of bread and to prayer.
> ACTS 2:42

Notice how the members operated under the authority of the apostles. The small groups meeting in homes were part of a much larger movement, not independent fiefdoms. As a result, there was unity within the groups and in the church as a whole. Leaders saw themselves as extensions of the apostles' ministry. They taught in line with the teachings of the apostles. They led their small groups as the apostles instructed. They operated under the authority of these men.

The writer of Hebrews reiterated this same principle some years later:

> Have confidence in your leaders and submit to their authority, because they keep watch over you as those who must give an account. Do this so that their work will be a joy, not a burden, for that would be of no benefit to you.
> HEBREWS 13:17

Though the authorship is unknown, I believe that Apollos wrote the letter to the Hebrews. He served in Corinth and understood well the problems created by disunity in the church. When small groups act independently or verbally oppose the church's leadership, the church's ministry suffers. Small groups must operate under the umbrella of church leadership.

### 2. Support your leaders in group discussions and private conversations

As a small group leader, you serve as an extension of the church's pastors, elders, deacons, and other leaders. Therefore, you must fully support and champion the overall ministry of the church. Never allow discussions in your small group meetings to drift into negative comments about the pastors and other leaders. Redirect conversations when they begin to head in that direction. Don't allow your small group to be a place for gossip.

You may have members who attend your small group meetings but refuse to worship with the larger church body. If so, challenge those individuals. Speak positively about the worship services. Share with the group how the Lord used the larger gathering to speak to you or encourage you. Talk about the sermon. After a while, those who have not attended worship may feel they are missing out.

Notice what Paul wrote to Timothy, a young pastor and his son in the faith, on this matter:

> The elders who direct the affairs of the church well are worthy of double honor, especially those whose work is preaching and teaching.
>
> I TIMOTHY 5:17

Honoring leadership is vital to the overall health of your church and small group ministry. In every public and private conversation, demonstrate your support for those working to lead the ministry. Modeling this attitude in front of your group is essential to set the right tone in your meetings.

### 3. Address issues with leaders individually, not in your small group

There may be times when you disagree with a decision a leader has made. Church members will never have perfect unity on every issue. Any church with zero disagreements is a church with only one member. Conflict is inevitable and should be expected.

However, healthy churches understand the correct way to handle conflict. As a leader and example to others, you must model the right way to address disagreements.

In Matthew's Gospel, we read the words of Jesus on how to address a brother or sister in Christ who falls into sin:

> If your brother or sister sins, go and point out their
> fault, just between the two of you. If they listen to you,
> you have won them over. But if they will not listen, take
> one or two others along, so that "every matter may be
> established by the testimony of two or three witnesses."
> If they still refuse to listen, tell it to the church; and if
> they refuse to listen even to the church, treat them as you
> would a pagan or a tax collector.
> MATTHEW 18:15-18

While Jesus specifically addresses personal sin, I believe this passage provides a model for handling most disagreements. Therefore, following the instructions of Jesus, here are the steps you should take in handling any conflicts you have with leaders in your church:

1. *Go directly to your pastor or other leaders with your concern.* In my experience, 95 percent of conflicts can be resolved with this first step. Two Christ followers who take the time to privately and humbly discuss a concern will almost always find a resolution.

   Years ago, a small group leader contacted me about my absence from our annual volunteer appreciation event. His concern was valid. This is the time every year when I can personally and publicly say "thank you" to our most committed members and those who work in our various ministries each week. But this particular year, I didn't attend the event. Months before, I had made plans to be out of town with my wife. When our pastoral staff looked at the calendar, the only available date for the volunteer appreciation event happened to conflict with my already-paid-for, nonrefundable, and badly needed vacation. After much debate, I allowed our staff to plan this gathering at a time most convenient for our volunteers rather than accommodate my personal schedule.

   When I explained this to the small group leader who had contacted me, he agreed that I'd made the right decision. The issue was resolved. Conflict was avoided.

   However, imagine if this group leader had dealt with his concern another way. What if he'd grumbled about my absence in front of his small group? Or what if he'd shared with several friends his opinion that I was less than supportive of our volunteers? Imagine how those sentiments could have bled into the hearts and minds of other leaders.

Eventually, a nonissue would've become a considerable problem in our church, causing our ministry to suffer.

Go to the pastor or other leader directly with questions or concerns, and you'll solve almost every conflict.

If for some reason this first step doesn't resolve the problem, you can go to step 2.

2. *Ask another trusted leader to help mediate the situation.* Let's suppose you address your concerns directly to the other person, but at the end of the meeting you still haven't reached a resolution. A discomfort remains in your heart and mind. Depending on the exact nature of the problem, you may want to ask the leader if this issue can be discussed with a few other individuals. Perhaps the two of you could pull in a couple of other small group leaders and see if they have any insight. Or maybe you want to ask one or two elders or deacons to meet and talk through the matter. Again, most of the time, the conflict never rises to this level; however, if it does, having several leaders in the church discussing and praying through the matter will almost certainly bring resolution.

While 95 percent of all issues can be solved at the first step, probably 99 percent are solved by the end of step 2. If leaders on both sides are humble and honest, it's rare that a disagreement can't be resolved after following the first two steps. But if it isn't, you still have another step you can take.

3. *Choose to let it go or step down.* If you go through steps 1 and 2 and are still uncomfortable with the decision the leaders have made, you essentially have two options. The first is to say, "Though I disagree with this decision, God has called these individuals to lead our church. Therefore,

I will put my opinions aside and follow their leadership." The second option is to say, "This decision runs so contrary to my beliefs that I cannot serve under these leaders. Therefore, I'm going to step down from my role as a small group leader."

Again, this situation is extremely rare if you are serving in a church with like-minded Christians. You have the same beliefs about the gospel. You agree on fundamental theological truths. The much less consequential decisions about exactly how to structure the church's ministry can generally be negotiated with minimal conflict if both parties have the church's best interest in mind.

Let me reiterate how important it is to follow these steps. This is a critical element of the church's health. Your role in this is vital. Your church will grow and affect the Kingdom if you live this out. Gossip, passive-aggressive comments, and other methods of undermining leaders are not healthy and will only cause greater disunity.

As the leader of your small group, you are the pacesetter in fostering unity. Your boots-on-the-ground conversations and attitudes are invaluable to your church. Although this may be tough in some situations, your work in this area will make a difference in the lives of your group members and in the effectiveness of the gospel in changing lives in your community.

It's well worth the effort.

# 4

# Rules of the Game

*Establishing Expectations for Your Group*

IN SO MANY WAYS, expectations are the key to life. If you're married, you know this truth very well. If your spouse expects you to be home by nine o'clock, and you come walking in at ten thirty, you'll spend the rest of your evening explaining and arguing.

If your spouse expects you to be home at eleven, and you come walking in at ten thirty, you'll likely be greeted with, "Oh, you're home early. How was your evening, honey?"

Your arrival time was the same in each scenario. Your actions didn't change. What made the difference, then, between an evening spent arguing and a pleasant welcome home greeting?

Expectations.

This is true across all areas of life. In our friendships, in our workplaces, on sports teams, with our children, and in virtually every aspect of our lives, expectations often dictate our responses to the words and actions of others. When reality lines up with what we thought would happen, we're usually happy. Conversely, when what happens diverges from what we expected, discontentment and conflict may soon follow.

Therefore, it is critical to establish a set of ground rules for group members during the early stages of your small group. Developing a framework for the group's behavior and communicating those expectations will go a long way toward ensuring a positive experience for all.

At your first meeting, have everyone write their top three expectations for the group on an index card. Even if your group has been together for months or years, you can easily do this at the beginning of a semester or new year. Allow everyone to do this anonymously. Collect the cards, compile the list, and present the answers to the group.

Everyone will have different expectations. Some responses will signal a desire for friendship and care. Others will indicate a hunger to learn more about the Bible. A few will express hope that your group will be a safe place to talk about their lives. You may see expectations about spending time praying for one another, or finding a spiritual mentor, or learning how to be a better spouse or parent. You might even have some cards returned to you with a big question mark. Members may have joined the group not really knowing what to expect.

Most of the expectations expressed on the cards will be in line with your goals for the group. If someone writes, "I expect the members of this group to cut my grass each week and pay for my child's private school education," that would be a good time for you to explain the purpose of the group. However, that is highly unlikely. Expectations will generally fit with the marks of a healthy group we discussed in chapter 2.

After reviewing the list with your group, you might say something like this: "In order to meet these goals, we must establish a few ground rules. For everything to work, we need to make several commitments to one another. Let's create a covenant regarding how our group will operate."

Then take time to lead your group through a discussion of the following areas: attendance, confidentiality, respect, prayer, and format. Of course, you may want to add more items to the list; but the following items will give you some ideas about what to cover and allow your group members to come to a consensus on how everyone will relate to one another.

## Attendance

Whenever I ask small group leaders about their greatest challenges, the number one answer has to do with sporadic attendance. One leader shared with me his frustrations:

> I spend time studying the material and developing questions. I pray for each small group member. My wife buys desserts and makes coffee. We get our house cleaned and ready. We do all these things only to have some group members send me a text thirty minutes before the meeting letting me know they won't be there because their adult daughter just dropped in with the grandkids. I understand things coming up at the last minute, but can't you tell your daughter and grandkids that you'll see them later? That you've made a commitment to be at your small group?

A lack of real commitment seems to be the way of our society. We have so many options to fill our time. No one wants to commit to anything, just in case something better comes along.

However, as a society, our attendance records are stellar at some events, meetings, and appointments. If something is high on our priority list, we will move heaven and earth to be there.

I recently served as a coach for my ten-year-old son's baseball team. There were twelve players and three coaches on this team (a perfect size for a small group). We played eight games during the summer season, and not one player or coach missed a game. A few games were moved to an alternate date and time because of rain. Every team member's family adjusted their schedule to make sure their son was at the game. Why?

It was a priority.

Say to your group members, "I know everyone is busy. And I know things come up. However, let's set a time when most people can prioritize being here. For the success of our small group, we need to keep this commitment to one another."

## Confidentiality

Some things should not be shared outside of the group. At your ground rules meeting, establish the need for confidentiality among your group members. Obviously, not everything must be held in the strictest confidence. If a member shares that her son is the valedictorian of his class, it's most likely okay to share that information with others outside of your group. However, certain statements must remain within the confines of your small group.

Years ago, I led a small group of teenage guys. At one of our meetings, the boys shared some of their personal battles with temptation. Later, I spoke with a fellow staff pastor and mentioned these issues in a very general way. I gave no names or details, just the big picture of certain struggles among teenagers and how it affected families in our church. I thought he understood that this wasn't something he needed to broadcast, but rather information that would be helpful as he ministered to church members.

I was wrong.

He filled in some of the particulars and used it as a sermon illustration on a Sunday he was asked to preach. I wanted to melt into my seat. I immediately went to these teenagers, confessed my sin, and explained that I'd given no names or specifics; however, it was no excuse. I was clearly in the wrong and needed to keep our group discussions within the group.

I appreciate tremendously the confidentiality within my current small group. I've shared stories and struggles that I didn't want spread to the entire church. Don't judge me. You have plenty of things in your life you'd rather not see posted on Instagram. It's important to me that our small group is a safe place to talk.

Discuss with group members the parameters for confidentiality. Emphasize the need to abide by the guidelines your group establishes. A few words spoken out of the proper context will not only hurt one of the members but will destroy trust within the group as well.

## Respect

Lead your group members through a discussion about expectations for interacting with one another. Establish certain ground rules on how you will speak to each other in your meetings.

I made the mistake of not doing this with a group I led early in my ministry. There were two members of our small group who didn't get along—the wife of one couple and the husband of another. Good thing they weren't married to each other. How they ended up in the same group, I have no idea.

Most of the group members were unaware of the animosity between these two until one particular evening. The woman made a passive-aggressive comment about something the man had said. His response was far more aggressive than passive. No one else said a word. A thick, suffocating silence blanketed the room. After a minute (which felt like an eternity), the guy ended up walking out of the meeting. His wife stayed, looking extremely uncomfortable and unsure about her next move. I quickly said, "Let's pray and end a little early tonight." I then made a joke about wanting to get home in time to watch the latest episode of *Lost*; however, everyone in the group knew exactly why we cut our time short.

The group fizzled not long afterward. No one wants to attend an awkward meeting. Life is too short.

Suggest to your group something like this: "We will not belittle the opinions of others. We might disagree; however, we can do so in a manner that is courteous and kind. Furthermore, we will not interrupt each other. We will allow others to speak freely."

Then ask the group for other suggestions for how members can best show respect to one another. Finally, lead the group to a consensus on this issue so that expectations for proper behavior will be clear from the beginning.

## Prayer

Start this discussion by saying, "One of the best ways we can care for and encourage one another is through prayer, both in our meetings and throughout the week. We should pray not just when we are sick or have some other tangible need. We need to pray for one another's spiritual growth, for our children to grow strong in the Lord, that we will have opportunities to share the gospel, and that the Lord will protect our lives and families from spiritual attack."

Ask your group for their thoughts on the best way to pray for one another. There may be a member who would like to coordinate this effort and send reminders. Or perhaps the group members will rotate through the names of the others in the group and pray for them on different days of the week.

One leader shared a story about a member disclosing to the group that he and his wife were having a lot of trouble with one of their college-age children. The wife cried quietly as the husband shared the details of their son's recent revelations of drug use. Moreover, this son refused to cooperate with them as they attempted to help him separate from friends and leave this lifestyle. They were heartbroken.

According to the leader, the news of this teenager's activities was a shock to the group. He was a sweet kid from a good family. Several had served as his Sunday school teachers or as leaders during his time in the student ministry. They couldn't believe he'd traveled down this rebellious path.

This situation reminds me of our need to cover one another with prayer *before* a crisis occurs, not just after the bad news comes to our attention.

What would happen if your group committed to praying for one another regularly and consistently? What if your prayers went beyond, "Bless us and keep us safe"? What if members pledged to pray for God's spiritual protection over each other's children, each other's marriages, each other's lives? What if you prayed for spiritual growth for other group members, and they prayed for you as well? Can you imagine how the Lord would work in your small group and in your church?

Lead your group in discussing the best way to organize prayer for one another. Again, there may be a member who loves spreadsheets and would be happy to devise a prayer calendar and email reminders to the group. Ask for ideas about how best to organize this effort and develop a plan.

## Format

The members of your group will need to agree on the format for your meetings. If your group is a class that meets on Sunday mornings before or after a worship service, many of the details may already be decided for you. But you still should discuss how your meetings will be structured. Certainly if your group meets outside of Sunday morning, your group will need to answer several questions:

1. *Will your group be open or closed?* Unless your church has already made this decision for you, you will need to determine this important boundary. Let's look at some definitions.

    If your group is *open*, members are allowed—and perhaps encouraged—to invite others into the group at any time. These could be guests visiting for one meeting or individuals looking to join the group permanently. Open groups may have a focus on outreach or assimilation within your church. The trade-off is that openness creates a level of uncertainty about who will be present at group meetings, and over time it may keep the group from sharing more deeply with one another.

    If your group is *closed*, members are not allowed to invite anyone new into the group without consulting with the other group members. Closed group meetings are more predictable and may foster a higher sense of commitment and accountability. Also, as members get to know each other over time, a level of trust may develop that will allow for a deeper level of sharing. New members may still be added, but only with the agreement of the members. Finding that a group is closed can be off-putting to newcomers who are looking for a place to connect, so be prepared to refer inquirers to another group that might have room for new members.

Define both of these types of groups for your members and decide which format everyone finds preferable.

2. *Will you eat together as a group?* If so, who will provide the food? Some groups structure their meetings like a "supper club" by rotating who brings dinner each week. This allows the members to spend the first hour sitting around a table together and talking. To ensure that there is the right amount of food, group members are asked to RSVP, which discourages members from choosing not to come at the last minute.

3. *What day and time will the group meet?* Will you meet each week or every other week? Who will coordinate sending out reminders about the meetings?

4. *How long will the meetings last?* Members need to know when to expect the meetings to end, especially if they have children with a babysitter at home.

5. *Where will the group meet?* Will it be in someone's home, or will you rotate homes? Will you meet on the church campus? If so, who will be responsible for coordinating this with the appropriate staff member at the church?

6. *What will be the format for the studies?* Will you use teaching videos? Will you read a book together? If so, should

members have portions of the book read before coming to the meeting? Will you rotate who is responsible to lead the discussions, or will one person primarily lead?

As you review these questions with your group, your members may express and define additional expectations. This does not necessarily need to be a long process, but these questions should be discussed at an early meeting and a consensus formed.

I don't recommend using a written covenant. It seems too formal and may be intimidating, especially to those who are new to the idea of being in a small group. You can have more of a handshake agreement, but that doesn't mean you won't have group expectations. Feel free to send a follow-up email outlining the parameters discussed. This will serve as a reminder as well as bring clarity.

Ultimately, you want your small group to be a positive experience for everyone. Establishing expectations early on will help make this possible.

# 5

# Getting Ready

*Selecting Studies and Preparing for Your Meetings*

"WOULD YOU LIKE to preach for me next Sunday?"

The question caught me off guard. I was fresh out of college and preparing to begin my seminary training. Not only that, but it was my first week in my new role as student pastor when the senior pastor approached me. I had little experience speaking in front of groups of any size and had zero experience preaching on a Sunday morning before a crowd of several hundred. I could feel my body stiffen when he asked the question. A voice in my head screamed, "No!"

However, for some strange reason, my tongue refused to follow the orders of my central nervous system. Perhaps it was my people-pleasing nature wanting to endear myself to my new employer. Or maybe a quadrant of my brain knew that a call to the ministry meant I would eventually need to become comfortable preaching in a worship service. Whatever the reason, the next words out of my mouth were, "Sure, Pastor, I'd be happy to preach for you."

He smiled and thanked me. As he walked away, my first thought was, *Oh no. Now what? I've agreed to preach, but what am I going to say?*

You may have a similar feeling now that you've agreed to lead a small group. People have joined your group. You've selected a day, a time, and a location. You've emailed or texted the members about the upcoming meeting. You've made arrangements for food and childcare.

Now what?

The members will gather at your home, another member's house, a specified room at the church, or some other location. Individuals and couples will arrive, introduce themselves, grab food or drink, and engage in small talk. After a while, these group members will look to you for whatever comes next. They will expect you to lead them in a group meeting or Bible study.

What are you supposed to do?

Though this is far from an exhaustive list, here are several ways to prepare for that first group meeting:

## Select a Study

Perhaps your pastor or another church leader has already provided the study material for your group. If this is the case, then obviously the decision has been made for you.

However, if it's up to you to decide, ask yourself the following questions:

- What is a common need of our group members?
- What am I comfortable teaching or leading?

- Will my group members read a book, or do I need to select a video series?
- Should we do a topical study or study a book of the Bible?

After you answer these questions, consider your options and spend some time praying through each of them. Ask the Lord to direct you to the study that will most benefit your group. *Don't skip this step.* You'll be amazed at how the Lord will reveal what you need to do.

One leader in our church told me about a time when the Lord clearly directed him to choose a particular study. As he prayed through his options, he felt as if his group needed to do a series on marriage. This study required them to divide into two groups. Husbands would go to one room and wives to another. This was a first for his group, and the first time his wife would be leading. They discussed this option, prayed through it, and ultimately decided to try this format and study for the next semester.

Little did they know that a couple in their group had recently separated and were strongly considering divorce. They'd planned on dropping out of the small group; however, when the leader announced the topic and that husbands and wives would be going through the study separately, this couple agreed to attend the meetings. They showed up individually to the home. They were cordial but cool with each other. Their future together seemed very uncertain.

The members of this small group prayed fervently for the couple. The men listened to the husband talk about his marriage struggles. They offered words of love and encouragement. They encircled him and prayed for him, his wife, and their marriage.

The women, meeting in a room on the other side of the house, did the same with the wife. They listened to her and prayed with her. They offered their support. They hugged her and cried with her.

You can likely guess what happened next. After a few weeks, the wall of hostility between this couple began to crumble. They agreed to meet with a counselor. After a few more weeks, the husband returned to their home. Their almost-broken marriage was restored.

All of this happened because a small group leader spent time praying before selecting the study for his group.

## Determine How Much Time You'll Have

As previously mentioned, you'll need to establish an end time with your group. Don't feel the need to be too rigid on this. If a member is pouring out his or her soul to the group, there's no reason to interrupt and call, "Time!" If the discussion is good and you get a sense from the other members that it's okay to go a little longer than usual, that is perfectly acceptable.

Even so, plan to end on time. To do this, you need to read through the study or watch the video. You can't always control how long discussions will last; however, you don't want to show a thirty-minute video if you know it will send you over your normal ending time. If you plan to go longer, communicate this information with the group members prior to the meeting and make it clear that anyone needing to leave on time is free to go.

## Review the Material

You're not expected to be the expert on every topic. However, you must be familiar with the material you are studying. If it's a video, watch it beforehand. If it's a book study, read the chapter before you meet with your group. If it's a book of the Bible, do some basic research on the book and read through the passages you'll be studying with your group. The better prepared you are, the easier it will be to lead the group sessions.

Don't feel as if you have to know every answer. If someone asks a question and you're unsure about the correct response, throw it back to the group: "What do the rest of you think about this question?" Someone in your group may very well offer a great insight.

I've made the mistake of not preparing beforehand. Leading and speaking before a group are nerve-racking in and of themselves; however, the less prepared you are, the more nervous you'll be. Don't try to wing it. Take some time to read and study before your group meets.

## Arrange the Room Well

This may sound odd or unimportant to you; however, the environment has a tremendous effect on the dynamics of your discussion. For example, let's say your group meets in a classroom on your church campus. When you walk in, the room is set up with a lectern at the front and six rows of seven chairs each. Your small group members will enter the room and choose a seat. Spouses will probably sit together, but most people are likely to leave several spaces between themselves and other members. Facing the front, where you're standing, they will be looking at the backs of other people's heads, while people seated behind them will be out of their sight.

With your environment alone, you've discouraged community and discussion. This seating arrangement will turn your small group meeting into a lecture, and you'll be expected to fill the time with your words.

Conversely, imagine walking into a room with only twenty chairs, all arranged in a large circle. If there are twelve members of your group, you've allotted enough seating for the men to sit directly next to their wives, yet still leave a seat between themselves and another man (hint: men hate sitting directly next to each other unless both are in recliners). You've also eliminated the front of the room as a focal point and shifted the perspective of your group toward discussion and group participation. You're now more likely to be viewed as the group's facilitator rather than the teacher. The environment suggests inclusion, equality, and the expectation that everyone will contribute.

If possible, I highly encourage you to have comfortable, living-room-style seating. If your small group meets in someone's home, this is a slam dunk. If you're meeting on your church's campus, you might have to ask a pastor or staff member for assistance. Ideally, the room you use will have sofas, coffee tables, lamps, and other home-type decor. This will create a relaxed atmosphere where individuals feel more comfortable sharing their ideas with the group.

## Pray for Your Group Members

Don't ignore this step. Throughout the week, spend some time each day praying for the members of your group and for the meeting itself. True spiritual change happens when the Holy Spirit works on people's hearts. The time you spend in prayer for your group members is one of the greatest gifts you can give them.

In Luke 11, immediately after Jesus teaches his disciples how to pray, he offers an object lesson about the importance of persistence in prayer. He poses a question about a man who has a friend visit him in the middle of the night. This friend has come from out of town and needs a meal and a place to stay. The host desperately wants to offer his tired, road-weary friend something to eat, but he has no food. So the man goes to a neighbor and asks for some bread to feed his friend. But what if the neighbor refuses?

Jesus says, "Suppose the one inside answers, 'Don't bother me.

The door is already locked, and my children and I are in bed. I can't get up and give you anything'" (Luke 11:7).

But the man doesn't leave. Instead, he continues to knock and ask until the grumpy, sleepy-eyed neighbor relents and gives the man bread for his friend.

Now, without getting too deep into the theological weeds, let's apply this parable to your small group situation. Who would the characters represent? The host is you, the neighbor is God, and the traveling friend represents your small group members. The bread symbolizes their needs—spiritual, physical, and relational. By praying persistently for your group members, you are like the friend going to the neighbor in the middle of the night, asking for bread to feed your friends.

Jesus encourages us to pray continually for the needs of others. This is one of the greatest gifts you can give your small group members and one of the best ways you can prepare for your meetings. Intercede to the Lord on their behalf, and then watch what the Lord does in their lives.

# 6

# But Nobody's Talking!

*How to Lead a Group Discussion*

"WHEN HAVE YOU heard God speak to you?"

This question changed the tenor of our small group meeting. Though I don't recall the exact passage or topic we were discussing, I remember well the uncertainty I felt when I asked the group this question. I had no idea what to expect. Would they respond with blank stares? Would they squirm in their seats? Would someone try to redirect the conversation to a less personal subject? Or was I opening the door to some off-the-wall replies that would put us on theological thin ice?

Thankfully, none of those things happened. Instead, one by one, the group members shared powerful stories of times when they had heard God speak. One guy, David, talked about a day he was water-skiing on a lake and sensed a voice telling him to let go of the rope. As he descended into the water, he looked to his right and saw a young boy signaling to him for help. Removing his water skis, David swam toward the shore, where the boy continued to wave and shout. Eventually it became shallow enough to walk on the lake bottom, and soon his legs hit something solid. Reaching down below the surface, David pulled up a five-year-old girl, the young boy's little sister. She'd never learned how to swim and had wandered too far out into the lake just moments before David heard the voice telling him to let go of the rope. As he pulled the little girl to the surface, she immediately began coughing and gasping for air. David hauled her to shore and put her into the arms of her grandmother, who had come down from the house when she heard her grandson's screams.

"Are you sure it wasn't the voice of the young boy you heard?" someone asked.

"No way. This voice was deeper," David said, "and it was *internal*. But it was real, and I'm convinced it was the Lord speaking to me."

Others began to share their own stories with the group. Though less dramatic than David's, they were still very moving accounts of hearing God direct their paths. It was a powerful, memorable night. At our next several meetings, the conversations went beyond surface-level sharing, taking on a deeper, more spiritual tone. And the overall dynamics of our group changed. We began to challenge and encourage one another in ways we hadn't done before. That discussion about hearing God's voice became a turning point for our small group.

The potential impact of your group's discussions extends well beyond the book you're reading, the video you're watching, or the material you're presenting. Getting members to open up and share what the Lord is doing in their lives will play a pivotal role in establishing your group dynamics.

The challenge for you is how to lead these discussions.

Admittedly, this is more of an art than a science. This chapter will offer a few suggestions, but it will take some on-the-job experience to really teach you how to navigate these conversations. But take heart: The longer you lead a group, the more comfortable you will become in guiding group discussions.

Following are several issues you may potentially face during meetings.

## Navigating Hot Topics

There will be times when group members disagree about an issue. It could be over what the Bible teaches about homosexuality, predestination, the end times, or the role of women in the church. Some group members may have firm opinions on one or more of these topics, and the conversation can become tense as emotions play into the discussion. Throwing out the question, "Does God choose us or do we choose God?" might be the equivalent of tossing a live hand grenade into the middle of the room. Goodhearted, Jesus-loving individuals will disagree, and perhaps quite passionately. So how do you navigate sensitive topics in a group with diverse opinions?

### *Redirect the conversation*

Imagine your group is studying the fruit of the Spirit found in Galatians 5. You ask for examples of kindness. Someone expresses an opinion that voting for a particular political party is an act of kindness because that party cares about the poor, loves America more, or has a kinder platform. It suddenly feels as if the air has been sucked out of the room. There may be others in the group who strongly disagree with that individual's statement. They may also be wondering how the discussion suddenly took a turn from Galatians 5 to the upcoming election.

This is where you need to redirect the conversation quickly. Say something like, "While that may or may not be true, I think this passage focuses on how the Spirit produces kindness in us on a personal level. Can you think of ways you've seen this transformation happen in your own life?" With any luck, at this point another member of your group will jump in and assist you in refocusing the discussion.

If someone continues to steer the conversation down a divisive road, have a one-on-one meeting with that individual. This can be right before or after your group time. Make it casual but clear.

"Jim, I appreciate so much all that you contribute to this group, and I need your help. You have great political insights; however, most group members aren't as knowledgeable as you are regarding the latest news. Additionally, I want us to focus on how these verses change us personally rather than the application to our nation or what is happening in Washington, DC. Can you help me keep our discussions more focused?"

Take time to pray before you talk with Jim, and I'm sure the Lord will direct your words.

### Talk about the elephant in the room

If you know that your group will have differing opinions on a controversial topic, feel free to tackle the issue head-on prior to the start of your meeting. For example, let's say you're reading Ephesians 1, and you know that your group will face the question of predestination versus free will. Talk about the potential controversy before you read the passage. By identifying the upcoming tension, you'll release pressure from the room. Group members will expect to disagree and know that they have the freedom to do so. Moreover, you can begin the discussion by saying something like this: "There are people who love Jesus and hold opposing views on this topic." By being open about differences of opinion, you give your group members the freedom to disagree without feeling "less Christian."

But what if the topic is one where you feel that there is only one right view? Again, be up front with your group. Openly share your perspective and acknowledge that others in the room may disagree with you. You can even jokingly say, "And because this is a free country, you have every right to be wrong." Let the group know how you have based your perspective on Scripture, and invite members who disagree with you to present their side as well. Showing your cards early will lessen the tension in the room as you walk through controversial topics.

### Set ground rules

Again, before you begin the meeting, acknowledge that there may be disagreement on the topic you're about to discuss. Then say something like, "We can hold different opinions and still be kind to one another. The goal of our time together isn't to win an argument. Rather, we are here to learn and grow in our faith." You might even let the group know that you'll be acting as the referee and will pull a yellow or red card if necessary.

## The Sound of Silence

Most people in our culture today abhor silence. Think about how rare it is to have zero noise in your life. Aside from the ten minutes or so before you nod off to sleep, there are very few other moments during the day when you have complete silence. In the car, there's the radio. As you walk through a store, Muzak plays in the background. At your office, there's clatter from the copier, dings from your computer, and alerts from your phone. To sit quietly is indeed a challenge for most of us. In a crowd of people, it's nearly impossible.

When you pose a question to your group and no one offers an immediate reply, you'll find yourself tempted to fill the void with the sound of your own voice. Sure, you might be able to endure the silence for five or ten seconds, but by the eleventh second, your tongue will begin to wag almost involuntarily. "Okay, let me ask the question another way," you might say. Or, "Here's the answer I would give to that question."

Resist the temptation to fill the silence. Instead, let it hang there a little longer. If you're uncomfortable, others are as well. Eventually someone will speak up to relieve the tension. As they share with the group their thoughts about a topic or passage, they become vulnerable to the other group members and create an environment where life change is possible.

Be willing to endure the sound of silence. Don't be so quick to rescue the group.

## Controlling the Conversation Dominators

If certain members of the group tend to dominate the discussions, you may need to direct some questions to specific individuals (the non-talkers) to get their thoughts. Do this carefully and judiciously, however, because people generally don't like to be put on the spot. If the discussion dominators don't take the hint, you may need to have a private conversation with them. Say something like, "You contribute so much to this group; however, I'm worried that others aren't sharing because they know you'll answer the questions. They're letting you do all the heavy lifting. I believe other members of our group will grow spiritually through sharing their ideas; we need to give them the conversational space to do so."

By including discussion dominators in the mission, you're giving them a spiritual reason to refrain from answering every question. The vast majority of individuals will respond positively to this request and curtail the time they speak in group meetings.

## When it gets awkward

Group members need the freedom to be open and honest with each other. A goal of your small group should be to develop an authentic community. Meetings should be a safe place for individuals to talk about their needs, hurts, and feelings.

However, some members may take it too far, going beyond simple vulnerability and attempting to use the group time as a personal therapy session. As they share their concerns, tension fills the room while everyone else becomes highly uncomfortable and suddenly develops a keen interest in their shoes.

How do you, as a leader, navigate these awkward situations? Here are some ideas.

1. *Conduct a preemptive strike.* Let's say you plan to lead your group through a study on boundaries in relationships. You know that it may open the door to some past pain and hurt among the members. Perhaps some will want to share their experiences with the group. Let the group know that this particular study may lead to some emotional conversations. Those in the group should feel free to share anything that is appropriate for the setting. For example, a statement such as, "My parents abused me, and I've had difficulty forgiving them," is acceptable. However, sharing the details of that abuse should be done in a therapist's office.

   This same principle applies to revelations about one's sins. James tells us, "Confess your sins to each other" (James 5:16), but the level of confession and detail should correlate to the size, composition, and closeness of the group. For example, a married man who struggles with lust should confess that sin only to his wife (perhaps), to a counselor, or to a trusted friend. He doesn't need to share that information with an entire small group, especially if the group includes both men and women.

Walk through a few examples of how your members can be open and honest with one another in appropriate ways for the setting.

2. *Address issues one-on-one.* If members of your group consistently use the meetings as a time to dump their junk onto others, you'll need to have one-on-one meetings with these people. First, ask them specific questions about the issue or issues they've discussed. They will love the fact that you've taken an interest in their problems and that you're allowing them to talk. After they've shared with you, mention some resources for them to consider. Perhaps a pastor or a therapist. If there is an organization such as Celebrate Recovery in your area, you may want to point them in that direction. Then end the conversation by saying, "I'm so glad that you've been open about your issues and you're willing to work through these problems. However, I would appreciate it if you would not reveal so much detail in our group meetings. What you're dealing with is pretty heavy and beyond what most members of our group can handle."

3. *Say, "Let's talk afterward."* You may need to stop a confession or revelation midstream. If something seems inappropriate for the setting, interrupt politely and say, "Hey, can we push pause right there for now, but you and I talk privately after our time together? I think we can discuss this in more detail and come up with some ideas on

how you can best move forward." Be courteous but firm. Your job is to protect your group. Other members will stop attending if meetings become awkward because of one or two individuals.

Again, leading group discussions is an art and not a science. It's impossible to give step-by-step instructions for how to react to every possible scenario. However, as you think through the examples above, you'll be prepared to face the challenges that come your way.

# 7

# Planning to Pray

*Creating Intentional Time for Prayer*

It's still one of my favorite stories.

Several years ago, a leader sent me an email about a notable event in the life of his small group. This newly formed group consisted of six young couples. Their first study together was the book of James. As they neared the end of the epistle, they came across the following verses:

> The prayer offered in faith will make the sick person well; the Lord will raise them up. If they have sinned, they will be forgiven. Therefore confess your sins to each other and pray for each other so that you may be healed. The prayer of a righteous person is powerful and effective.
>
> JAMES 5:15-16

They discussed this passage and the power of praying for one another. The conversation remained surface level for the first half of the meeting. Then a girl in the group shared her fears about facing an upcoming second surgery on her neck. Not only was she concerned about the procedure, but she and her husband were worried they'd have trouble paying the bills for this additional surgery.

The leader asked if the group could pray for her. They went around the room, praying in turn for this young woman and the situation with her neck.

After someone voiced a final "amen," one of the other members expressed a concern of his own. For months, he and his wife had been discussing his need for a new job, one that would give him more time in the evenings to be home with his young children. He'd applied for numerous positions, but nothing had worked out. He and his wife were worried that nothing ever would, and he would be stuck where he was.

Again, the group took time to pray. They went around the room, and everyone lifted up this young father and his need for a different job.

After the last person prayed, another man asked for prayer. He was in graduate school and struggling through a class. The professor had given an impossible assignment, one that threatened this young man's ability to complete his degree. The group paused to intercede for him.

Finally, a wife gave her husband an apprehensive look. After a few seconds, he shrugged his shoulders and said, "Okay, go ahead." With tears in her eyes, she told the group about their struggle with infertility. They'd been to numerous doctors and had come to the end of their options. Their next step was adoption; however, they still very much hoped to get pregnant.

The group prayed again. This time the members gathered around the couple, laid hands on them, and pleaded with the Lord on their behalf.

When the meeting ended, they all promised to continue praying for one another each day.

The following week, they gathered for their regular meeting. Before beginning the Bible study, the wife with the neck problem said, "Hey, thank you so much for your prayers. I had a scan this week, and the doctor told me I wouldn't need a second neck surgery after all. God must've healed my neck because a month ago, he assured me that I needed to go under the knife again. I really appreciate all of you praying for me."

Everyone chimed in with their excitement about this news.

"Well," the husband who was looking for a new job said, "you guys aren't going to believe this, but since we met last week, I've gotten a job offer. It's one that I really wanted, and it allows me to be home in the evenings. I've been struggling for months to find something else, and then after we prayed last week, this door opened. Thank you all for praying."

The group members all smiled, excited for this husband and feeling the importance of the moment. In just a week, two of the four prayers were answered.

"You've got to be kidding me," said the husband in grad school. "Remember how you prayed for me and the impossible obstacle I faced in my class? The professor changed the assignment. I felt a huge weight lift from my shoulders. I can't believe she made the change, but it means now I'll be able to graduate. Thank you all so much for your prayers."

By this point, everyone had chill bumps.

Finally, someone looked over at the couple who was trying to start a family and said dramatically, "Well, do you guys have any big news for us?" Everyone laughed. The laughter then turned to screams of joy when the wife smiled and said, "We just found out I'm pregnant."

In just one week, they had gone four-for-four with their prayer requests. Their leader later told me, "No one imagined that we'd have all our prayers answered, and so quickly. Looking back, I wish we'd added more requests to our list!"

What do you think happened to the faith of these group members after this experience? In case you're unsure, I can tell you: It grew tremendously. Those answered prayers became stakes in the ground. Years later, I still occasionally hear one of those individuals talk about that evening in their small group.

I wish every group would have this kind of experience.

Too often, our group meetings open and close with perfunctory, weak prayers.

*"Thank you for letting us be here together."*

*"Lord, just be with us today."*

*"Keep us safe and bring us back together next week."*

Can you point to one of those prayers being answered and growing your faith as a result? For example, if the Lord protected your group members and they all returned safely the following week, would that be a story you'd want to share with others? Would your faith in God explode as a result of every group member showing up to the meeting unharmed?

Probably not.

Reread this verse from Acts about the early church's small group meetings:

> They devoted themselves to the apostles' teaching and to
> fellowship, to the breaking of bread and to prayer.
> ACTS 2:42

Notice that they *devoted* themselves to prayer. Prayer was not an afterthought for these early Christians. They spent considerable time intently praying for one another.

It is entirely appropriate to pray, "Lord, keep us safe and bring us back together next week." Such a prayer acknowledges our dependence on God. However, it packs very little punch as a faith builder. It sort of skips along the surface of prayer. A group that *devotes themselves* to prayer goes deeper.

Are you leading your group to pray intentionally together? Here are a few ways you can make prayer a higher priority among your group:

1. *Divvy up and pray.* Most people find it intimidating to pray aloud in a group with more than a few people. However, if you divide the group (perhaps by gender), praying with three or four other individuals is not quite as nerve-racking. If you are meeting in a home, you may be able to send part of your group to another room in the house to pray together.

   Dividing up the group will not only create smaller groups in which people are more likely to voice their prayers, but they may also be more likely to open up and share needs they would otherwise keep to themselves. This is especially true if you group by gender. A subgroup may provide a more appropriate place to share a particular struggle than the entire group would.

2. *Challenge your group to rethink their prayer needs.* Prayer requests among American Christians tend to be limited to immediate needs. Too often, our prayers are along the same lines as the three wishes we would ask the genie

from *Aladdin*. "Lord, give me this, and this, and a little of that. In Jesus' name, amen."

There is nothing wrong with praying for physical, relational, or financial needs. I do it often. However, we need to think beyond the material world and pray for the spiritual needs all around us. When Paul wrote his letter to the Colossians, he asked them to "pray for us, too, that God may open a door for our message, so that we may proclaim the mystery of Christ, for which I am in chains" (Colossians 4:3). Challenge your group members to pray similarly.

3. *Ask someone to record the prayer requests and any answers.* You don't necessarily need to both lead the group and keep up with all the requests. I'm sure a member of your group would be willing to write down the prayer needs mentioned and then ask for updates each time you meet. As prayers are answered, this individual can record those as well. After your group has been meeting for several months, it might be worthwhile to go back and look at the requests and how God answered your prayers. It will encourage your faith and fuel your desire to "pray continually" (1 Thessalonians 5:17).

4. *Prepare a brief devotional thought on prayer.* In addition to your regular study, offer the group a few inspirational and instructional words before launching into your prayer time. This doesn't have to be a long lesson; rather, you can read a verse and offer a brief devotional thought before the prayer time.

You may want to assign this task to one of the other members (perhaps the same person recording the requests).

This will encourage others to focus their hearts and minds before talking to the Lord.

Consider using verses such as the following:

Pray in the Spirit on all occasions with all kinds of prayers and requests. With this in mind, be alert and always keep on praying for all the Lord's people.
EPHESIANS 6:18

Do not be anxious about anything, but in every situation, by prayer and petition, with thanksgiving, present your requests to God.
PHILIPPIANS 4:6

This is the confidence we have in approaching God: that if we ask anything according to his will, he hears us.
1 JOHN 5:14

Numerous other verses and passages address the importance of prayer.

Not every meeting will allow you to pray as a group for an extended period. However, as the leader, allow space for this on a regular basis. Intentional, focused prayers will grow the collective faith of your group.

# 8

# Coping with Conflict

*Dealing with Difficult Members*

WHEN PEOPLE BECOME followers of Christ, they become completely new creations (2 Corinthians 5:17). Their old way of life dies and is buried with Christ, and they are made to walk in a new life (Romans 6:4). Furthermore, at salvation, they receive the indwelling of the Holy Spirit (1 Corinthians 3:16). The Holy Spirit teaches them and guides them in their words and actions (John 14:26). As well, the Holy Spirit changes their character by producing love, joy, peace, forbearance, kindness, goodness, faithfulness, gentleness, and self-control (Galatians 5:22-23).

This is the new identity of those who have been saved and changed by the gospel.

But if it's true, why would we ever have any problems in our small groups? How in the world could there be conflict between two individuals who are controlled by the Holy Spirit? If the fruit of the Holy Spirit is love, peace, forbearance, etc., why would there ever be fights between church members?

Yet there are. If you've been involved in a local church for more than about five minutes, you've seen conflict. Why is this the case?

Generally speaking, there are three causes of conflict within churches and small groups:

1. *Christ followers can still operate out of the flesh.* Even though at salvation we become a new creation with a renewed spirit, we can still live according to our old nature. We can choose to walk in the Spirit or walk in our flesh. The apostle Paul writes about this in Galatians 5:16-26. Christians walking in the flesh often create conflict with other Christians.

2. *Christ followers are passionate about their church.* People tend to fight about the things they care about most. If your neighbor's son gets suspended from school, you're probably not going to be upset. However, if your own son gets suspended, you'll have trouble speaking calmly and rationally when you confront him about this news.

   Christians care about their church and the decisions made within the church. If they disagree with a decision, they will sometimes react passionately. Even Paul and Peter had a public fight over the issue of Peter's refusal to eat with Gentiles (Galatians 2:11-14). Our love for the church will, at times, cause us to have conflict with other Christ followers.

3. *There are non-Christians in our churches.* Perhaps even in your small group. Jesus emphasizes this point in a parable he tells in Matthew 13:24-30. In this passage, Jesus tells the story of a farmer sowing wheat in a field. During

the night, an enemy of the farmer comes and sows weeds. The next day, the farmer notices that wheat and weeds are both growing in his field. Jesus makes it clear that there will be unbelievers and believers coexisting in the church. Those who aren't new creations and who aren't controlled by the Holy Spirit will cause problems and create conflict in churches.

## Problem People

Even in very healthy small groups, there will be difficulties. You should expect problems and be ready to quickly address anything that steers your group in the wrong direction.

However, what is more challenging are *problem people*. Though every group can expect some level of conflict, there are occasions when groups become completely sidetracked by one individual or couple. From what I've observed, there are three categories of difficult members.

### Strange members

You may have individuals join your group who are just a little odd. They march to the beat of their own drum. When you throw out a question to the group, they will respond with an off-the-wall answer.

You: "What are ways that we can be salt and light to others?"

Them: "What about giving salt to my cat? I think she has rabies. I'm not sure."

Other group members will stare at you, waiting for your reaction. Some will simply roll their eyes.

These individuals usually are harmless. There are times they may drain you as a leader; however, they typically will not destroy your group. These members will need a little extra attention and some gentle correction, but rarely will they keep your group from fulfilling its purpose.

### Secret agenda members

These individuals want to take the group in a different direction. For example, they might be passionate about a particular theological issue. They see it as their mission to convert group members to their point of view. They will first target you, the leader, with suggestions for studies. If they have trouble getting you to convert to their theological position, they will start having individual conversations with other group members. If they can get others to align with them, this individual will come back to you and say, "So-and-so and I have met, and we agree on this, and we think you need to teach this study to the group." If they feel they can't get traction with you, they will begin to steer the group discussions to their way of thinking.

Depending on the nature and extent of the secret agenda member's views, this individual can be hazardous to the health of your group. The passion he or she has for their theological perspective may cause a rift between group members. Eventually, this conflict will seep out into the larger church body. Left unchecked, this member will destroy your group and cause significant damage to your church.

### Self-centered members

Self-centered members are in the group to get as much as they can out of the other people. They will suck you dry as a leader, and they will do the same to the other individuals in your small group. They will complain when their needs aren't met but not lift a finger when others need help.

Years ago, I had a small group leader call me about just such a couple. Their attitude was destroying the dynamics of the group. The leader confronted the husband, but to no avail. His wife had a difficult conversation with the wife of this couple, and still nothing changed. Finally, in desperation, the small group leader went to the other members and said, "We cannot continue to meet with this couple in our group. Therefore, I am dissolving the group and encouraging each of you to go and find another small group." It was his only choice.

I hope this section won't apply to you and your small group. Ideally, all who join your group will be sincere in their faith and genuinely desire a healthy group experience. However, if a problem person happens to join your group, what can you do? Here are a few suggestions for how to handle challenging individuals.

1. *Honestly address problems with the entire group.* This is slightly akin to the whole class at school having to forgo recess because of one disruptive kid. Or the entire team having to run laps because one player fumbled the ball. It doesn't quite seem fair, but it lets the other group members know you're not ignoring the problem.

    For example, you may open one of your meetings by saying something like this: "I know we veered off topic a few times during our previous study. Let's try to stay focused on the passage for this meeting. We'll have time to fellowship afterward, and we'll be able to talk about other things during that time." By doing this, you've put the individual who likes to derail the conversation on notice.

2. *Continually remind the group of the mission.* This may be part of your opening remarks at the outset of the meeting.

It's similar to the old high school football coach who was asked how he planned to win the big game on Friday night. "The main thing," he barked, "is to keep the main thing the main thing."

If you sense the group is getting off track, remind them of why you are together. Go back to the chapter on healthy groups and talk through those characteristics. Reiterate your primary purpose for meeting.

3. *Address disruptive individuals directly, kindly, and firmly.* If their behavior is only minimally disruptive, you can do this before or after one of your meetings. More severe situations will require a separate appointment. Talk honestly with this individual. For example, you may say, "John, I know that you are passionate about this theological issue, but that is not the belief of our church. I respect your view; however, you need to respect the position of our church as well. Please don't bring this up again in our meetings."

If John agrees, then it's a win, and you've successfully shepherded him and the group. If John becomes angry and leaves the group, then the problem is solved as well. If John stubbornly refuses to change or leave, you will have to resort to more dramatic measures.

4. *Pray hard.* Don't underestimate the power of prayer. Ask God to either change the unruly individual's heart or move him or her out of the group. Pray that God will open doors for you or other group members to talk to the person about the disruptive behavior. Ask him to protect your group from further damage. Spend time each day praying about this situation, and watch how the Lord answers your prayers.

5. *Appeal to a higher power.* We've already covered appealing to the *highest* power in step 4. It may also be helpful to take your problem to a pastor or other leader in the church. If the difficult member refuses to change, it is entirely appropriate to have another leader intervene. Depending on the severity of the situation, this leader may need to reassign the individual or couple to another group.

6. *Consider ending the group.* As a last resort, you may have to dissolve the group. This can be challenging, messy, and may feel like a failure on your part. However, there are occasions in life when separation is best for the ministry. Consider the situation between Paul and Barnabas in Acts 15:36-41. These two men fiercely disagreed over whether to include John Mark on their next missionary journey. Ultimately, they decided to go their separate ways.

   There are occasions when we must agree that our small group experience will be better for all if we're not in the same room. It doesn't necessarily mean that one individual is right and the other is wrong. Instead, it's that we are different. If your small group isn't healthy, it's better to end that group than to continue in an unhealthy manner.

I hope this chapter will be entirely irrelevant for you and your group. Though we are each flawed, broken individuals, I hope that all your group members will have the right focus and attitude in your meetings. Lord willing, this discussion will provide *perspective* and will not become your go-to chapter as a small group leader.

9

# On Mission

*Serving Together as a Small Group*

ONLY ONE OF Jesus' miracles appears in all four Gospels: the story of his feeding the five thousand. Matthew, Mark, Luke, and John all believed this event was important enough to include in their accounts of Christ's life. This is also likely the most widely known of Jesus' miracles. It's a story often read to children in Sunday school. The gathered crowd is hungry, and the only food available is a boy's sack lunch of two fish and five loaves of bread. Supplied with only this small meal, Jesus feeds five thousand men (and perhaps twice that many women and children) and still has twelve baskets full of food as leftovers.

There is, however, one detail that is often overlooked: Jesus *doesn't* feed the crowd.

Go to Matthew's version of the story:

As evening approached, the disciples came to him and said, "This is a remote place, and it's already getting late. Send the crowds away, so they can go to the villages and buy themselves some food."

Jesus replied, "They do not need to go away. *You* give them something to eat."

MATTHEW 14:15-16 (ITALICS ADDED)

Did you notice Jesus' response? When the disciples asked him to send the people away, he replied, "No, *you* give them something to eat." Jesus blessed the food, but the disciples were the ones who distributed it. Technically, the heading for this story shouldn't be "Jesus Feeds the Five Thousand," it should be "The *Disciples* Feed the Five Thousand."

Why is this important? Through their own service, the disciples saw Jesus do the miraculous. While they did what they could do (passing out food), Jesus did what only he can do (miraculously multiplying five loaves and two fish). As they obeyed the Lord's command, their faith in Jesus grew stronger.

Another well-known event in the life of Jesus and the disciples comes right on the heels of this miracle. Jesus tells the disciples to get into a boat and go to the other side of the Sea of Galilee. It is late in the evening, and as they begin to row the approximately eight miles across the lake, a storm suddenly appears. The wind and waves keep them from going any farther. As if a dark and stormy evening in a small boat in the middle of a large lake isn't scary enough, they then see what appears to be a ghost approaching from across the water. Just before they all have a heart attack, Jesus calls to them and says, "It is I" (Matthew 14:27).

I'm sure you know what happens next: "'Lord, if it's you,' Peter replie[s], 'tell me to come to you on the water'" (Matthew 14:28).

Jesus says, "Come," and Peter literally takes a bold step of faith. He gets out of the boat and walks on the water (Matthew 14:29).

Where did Peter get the kind of faith to obey this crazy summons from Jesus and attempt to do something so illogical?

Through the seemingly mundane act of serving fish and bread.

Only a few hours earlier, Peter had seen Jesus empower him and the other eleven disciples to miraculously feed a massive crowd. As Peter served, not only did the people have their bellies filled, but Peter's faith grew—to the point that, later the same evening, he was willing to step out of a boat onto roiling waves because he trusted Jesus that much.

This is a crucial principle for us today. If you want your small group members to grow in their faith, it will take more than just studying the Bible. True discipleship will happen only if they have opportunities to *serve*, both inside and outside the church. If your small group members gather each week, read the Bible, discuss questions, and pray together, but never serve in some capacity, they are missing a significant opportunity for faith building.

A failure of the American church is that we have fostered a system in which people are allowed to sit and soak it all in without any expectation of serving. This is why far too many churches are in decline and far too many Christians remain babies in their walk with the Lord. As a small group leader, you can work to change this mindset. Challenge your members to see themselves as the body of Christ on earth, vital to the success of the ministry. Don't expect just a few people to do the work of ministry, and certainly don't leave the work to paid professionals. If your church is going to prevail against the gates of hell and win the lost in your community, it will take everyone working and serving.

Moreover, as I mentioned earlier, your members miss a huge opportunity to grow in their faith if they fail to serve. They will

never fully mature by sitting and listening to sermons or partici-
pating in group discussions. Only when they actively *serve* in the
ministry will their faith grow to the point that they will trust Jesus
enough to get out of the boat and walk on water.

How can you lead your group members in looking for opportunities to serve? Here are a few suggestions.

## Model Serving

You are serving by leading a small group; however, there are other
ways to help the ministry of your church as well. For example,
working in the preschool or children's ministry, serving as a greeter,
or coming early on Sundays to assist in preparing and serving coffee are all opportunities to use your gifts.

Talk to your group about various ways to serve, and tell them
about the joy you find in serving. Let them know how they are
missing out if they don't volunteer. Foster excitement among your
group members about serving.

## Encourage Serving

Perhaps you could lead your group in a study about serving.
Teach the principle I mentioned earlier in the chapter, that serving is an essential ingredient to our spiritual growth. Pose questions about experiences others have had in serving and explain
how their faith grew as a result. Ask a leader in the church for a
list of volunteer opportunities and share that with your group. As
you do these things, you'll help create an expectation of service
in your group.

Several years ago, my wife and I visited a church in South
Carolina on a Sunday morning. As we pulled onto the church
campus from the main road, we noticed several individuals with
orange vests helping direct cars in the parking lot. From the

moment we turned into the parking lot until we pulled into a space, no fewer than ten individuals assisted us in knowing exactly where to park.

As we exited our vehicle, a friendly young man greeted us and asked if he could help. We told him we were visiting for the first time and weren't sure where to go. He walked us to a tent located outside the building. Underneath was a table with information about the church and four or five people wearing lanyards identifying them as volunteers. The parking lot attendant introduced us to another volunteer and told her that we were there for the first time. She asked us a few questions, answered ours, and walked us inside. Before we entered the worship center, someone else greeted us, gave us a bulletin, and helped us find seats. After the worship service, we wandered the building looking at their children's and student areas. We noticed dozens of individuals with T-shirts or lanyards identifying them as volunteers. Everywhere we went, these men and women asked if they could be of assistance to us.

What we witnessed as we meandered through their campus was, I'm sure, just the tip of the iceberg. I imagine many more volunteers were working in preschool classrooms, teaching the children, leading in worship, and serving in all the other areas of the church's ministry.

This church had managed to create a culture of serving. The vast majority of the membership came to church not to be served but to serve. That was clearly the expectation, and one the congregation had embraced.

If this is not the culture of your church, you can be a catalyst to help change the congregation's mindset. Perhaps your small group can lead the way in creating an expectation of serving among the greater church body.

## Serve Together

If your group meets on a Sunday morning, take a break one Sunday a month to serve in an area of your church. Coordinate this effort with your leaders, and communicate clearly with your group what will happen on that Sunday. For example, your members may need a background check before serving in your preschool, children's, or student areas. Give plenty of notice so that any logistical issues can be handled before the Sundays you are serving.

Additionally, you may want to encourage your group to serve at an event, such as a fall festival or other community outreach event. Our church sponsors an annual Christmas light festival for our city, and many of our small groups serve as greeters/ambassadors for the various nights of the light show. Often they will work for a couple of hours and then eat dinner together afterward.

You can choose many different options as you encourage your members to do more than just attend church and small group meetings, but to actively serve in your church's ministry. As your members serve, your church will expand its ministry, and your members will expand their faith. It's a win-win!

# 10

# Give It Away

*How to Train New Leaders*

I LOVE THE PRACTICAL insights taught in the Bible. Sure, the main purpose of God's Word is to show us the path of salvation. That's indisputable. The gospel is the primary truth we find in the pages of Scripture.

However, there are also many practical principles to be found in the Bible. Even an atheist would find valuable lessons in God's Word regarding work, marriage, relationships, money, and virtually every other aspect of daily life.

One of those principles is found in Exodus 18. After Moses led the people of Israel out of captivity in Egypt, he found himself in charge of a nation of people with no formal government or structure. Each day, he sat in a judge's seat and met with quarreling parties. From early in the morning until late in the evening, he rendered decisions on everything from mild disputes to severe conflicts. All the Israelites desired direct access to Moses for help in solving their problems. So day after day, all day long, Moses met with the people to decide on every life issue in Israel.

When Jethro, Moses' father-in-law, heard of this arrangement, he said to Moses:

> What you are doing is not good. You and these people who come to you will only wear yourselves out. The work is too heavy for you; you cannot handle it alone. Listen now to me and I will give you some advice, and may God be with you. You must be the people's representative before God and bring their disputes to him. Teach them his decrees and instructions, and show them the way they are to live and how they are to behave. But select capable men from all the people—men who fear God, trustworthy men who hate dishonest gain—and appoint them as officials over thousands, hundreds, fifties and tens. Have them serve as judges for the people at all times, but have them bring every difficult case to you; the simple cases they can decide themselves. That will make your load lighter, because they will share it with you.
>
> EXODUS 18:17-22

As one called by God, Moses believed he needed to do all the work. Older, wiser Jethro helped him see the error of his ways. If Moses continued in the same manner, he would burn out both himself and his people. He would become exhausted if he met all day long with opposing parties. The people would become frustrated by constantly having to wait to present their cases before Moses. The system was a lose-lose situation for everyone.

Wisely, Moses embraced Jethro's counsel. He chose capable

men to share in the leadership responsibilities. Newly appointed officials oversaw thousands, hundreds, fifties, and tens. Not only did these men lessen the burden on Moses, but they were also able to accomplish far more together than Moses could alone. Jethro's plan benefited everyone.

Far too often, American churches operate in a pre-Jethro system. They leave everything to the professionals—the pastors and paid ministry leaders. They hire experts to preach and teach while everyone else just listens and learns. As a result, most churches expect too little of their members.

*Come to worship.*

*Listen to a sermon.*

*Give if you're able.*

*No heavy lifting required.*

Sometimes this system persists because the members like being fed spiritually without having to do much else. Occasionally, the "one man show" exists because the pastor wants the church to operate that way. He enjoys being in charge. Either way, it is unfair to both the pastor and the church. Pastors burn out, and the effectiveness of the church is diminished. In my opinion, this is one of the reasons the average American church is dying.

Fortunately, your ministry doesn't operate this way. Your church has more of a Jethro model than a Moses model. How do I know this? You're a small group leader reading this book. Your pastor or another leader has appointed you to be one of the "capable men" to oversee a segment of the church membership.

Someone has given you the opportunity to serve as a shepherd of souls. They trust you that much.

However, it can't stop with you. You must be intentional about raising up other leaders.

Read what Paul wrote to the Ephesian church:

> Christ himself gave the apostles, the prophets, the evangelists, the pastors and teachers, to equip his people for works of service, so that the body of Christ may be built up.
>
> EPHESIANS 4:11-12

According to these verses, the degree to which the body of Christ (your church) will be built up depends on how many people are equipped for works of service. Therefore, training other individuals to do what you are doing will make your church more effective in reaching your community with the gospel.

If all the small group leaders in your church will commit to replicating themselves over the next year or two, you will double your reach and influence. Then imagine if all those new leaders reproduce themselves as well. What kind of impact would this have on your church and your community? How many lives would be changed for the better if every leader were to train one other individual to lead a small group of their own?

You can't control what other leaders do. But you can begin the process by training another individual to one day lead a group.

Here are several steps you can take to ensure that you are replicating yourself by teaching and training others to take leadership roles.

1. *Pray that the Lord will identify an individual as a candidate to train.* Every good and wise decision I've made began

with prayer. As you consider asking someone to step into the role of shepherding, you'll want to ask the Lord for discernment. While we focus on outward appearances, it is the Lord who looks at the heart (see 1 Samuel 16:7).

2. *Ask.* After praying and identifying a candidate, set up a time to meet with this individual over lunch or coffee. Share your thoughts and ask the person to pray about the possibility of leading a small group. You're not asking for a commitment right now, but let the person know that you would like to invest a year or two in focused training, with an eye toward eventually developing a new group leader.

3. *Offer opportunities to lead.* You might begin by allowing the person to teach and facilitate a meeting while you are there. Or divide your group in half for a series. You lead one half and allow the other person to lead the other half with your guidance.

4. *Debrief.* Find a time to meet with the candidate to offer feedback and answer questions. What went well? What didn't go well? What can be improved for next time?

5. *Let the person lead without you in the room.* Don't cancel your small group meeting if you're out of town or have some other conflict. Allow your assistant to fill in for you.

6. *Meet regularly for one-on-one training.* Study this book (or other small group training material). Schedule monthly meetings to talk through the issues covered in these chapters. How do you handle difficult members? What's the best way to guide discussions? Share your successes and failures. Talk honestly about frustrations, but also emphasize

the joy and privilege of serving the church and the Lord in this role.

Leaders training other leaders has been the key to the growth of our church. As mentioned in an earlier chapter, when I began my current ministry, we had only a handful of small groups. Initially, recruiting leaders for new groups was an incredible challenge. The old adage "beg, borrow, and steal" comes to mind when I think about how we convinced people to serve as small group leaders.

Over time, the task became far easier as existing leaders began to recruit and train other leaders. Every semester, we started new groups. Over the course of several years, we grew from only four or five adult small groups to nearly sixty. Sure, some of this growth happened because of church-wide initiatives; however, the multiplication occurred primarily because of individuals who were willing to replicate themselves. As experienced leaders invested in future leaders, our ministry grew in both breadth and depth.

Healthy churches recognize that the responsibility of ministry doesn't rest solely with the pastors, elders, or deacons. All who follow Christ are called to serve in some form of ministry. As you teach and model this principle, your church will make more and better disciples.

11

# Gimme a Break

*The When and Why of Not Meeting*

IMAGINE YOU ARE a senior in high school again, exploring your options for college. You pore over the websites of a dozen or more universities. You select five or six and go to these schools for official campus visits. You spend lots of time thinking, praying, and asking for advice from your parents and friends. Finally, you narrow your choice to two schools: State University and City College. You visit each school one more time to help you decide between the two. You travel to City College first and meet with an academic advisor.

"Tell me about your class schedule," you say.

"Certainly. We operate on the semester system. There is the fall semester, spring semester, and summer semester. We generally have a two- or three-week break between each semester."

You then travel to State University and meet with an official from that school. Again, you ask about the academic calendar.

"You'll begin your first year at State and go to classes each week until you finish your degree."

"What? No breaks at all? Not even for holidays?"

"No. Classes meet every week, fifty-two weeks a year. You'll get your break once you graduate."

Which school would you choose?

Our lives are structured far more like City College's academic plan than State's. We think in terms of semesters or quarters. Schools operate this way. Sports teams play for a season and take a break. We take time off from work for New Year's, Memorial Day, July 4th, Labor Day, Thanksgiving, and Christmas. It seems both illogical and unsustainable to work or take classes every week, all year long, without any breaks.

Moreover, you and I were designed by God to operate within the push and pull of work and rest. Notice what it says in Genesis 2:2-3:

> By the seventh day God had finished the work he had been doing; so on the seventh day he rested from all his work. Then God blessed the seventh day and made it holy, because on it he rested from all the work of creating that he had done.

The Lord certainly didn't rest because he was tired. He is an omnipotent being who doesn't need a day off to recharge his batteries. Instead, these verses are about God's *creation of rest* as part of the rhythm of life. Just as he created the heavens, the earth, animals, and humanity, he designed the aspect of life we call Sabbath. Before sin ever entered the world, Adam and Eve operated within this routine of work and rest.

Breaks are healthy and necessary in every part of life, including the life of your small group. If you are asking your members to commit to being present at your meetings, it's unreasonable to expect them to attend meetings every week of the year, year after year. Little else in our lives is structured this way. A healthy small group model will mirror the natural ebb and flow of our lives.

In my church, we have small groups we call Home Teams. They meet both on and off campus throughout the week, but not on Sunday mornings. We intentionally encourage all of our adults to join a Home Team, in part to give them the freedom to serve on Sundays. We have two morning worship services. In this model, adults are free to worship one hour, serve one hour, and attend a Home Team meeting during the week.

We advise our Home Team leaders to think "semesterly." Groups will typically meet from late August through the end of November, going through a specific study during this period. From Thanksgiving through the end of the year, most groups will not meet for their regular study. Typically, however, they will get together for a Christmas party or serve together in one of our Christmas outreach events.

Weekly group meetings resume from January through Easter, take another break, then meet for a "mini-mester" in May and June. This schedule offers rest for the leaders, the hosts, and the group members. It also increases the chances that members will be present for meetings during the semester.

We have a few adult classes that meet on Sunday mornings during our worship service times. We call these Connection Classes. These adults worship one hour and attend a class the second hour. Some of these classes are designed for people who are new to our church and want to learn more about following Christ or the church's vision. Additionally, there are a handful of other adult classes meeting on Sunday mornings.

Admittedly, the Sunday morning classes allow for more consistency in meeting. The vast majority of adults who participate in a worship service will attend their class every week they are in town. It's convenient. They don't have to navigate childcare issues. No one has to clean their home to prepare for the class.

Meeting every week throughout the year is more feasible in this model, but is it healthy? Even with this structure, allowing breaks for your group is beneficial. It allows the group an opportunity to serve together (see chapter 9) as well as end and begin a new study. Moreover, scheduling regular breaks will increase attendance during the semester. No one reasonably expects perfect attendance if you meet every week, all year long. By building in breaks (especially around typical vacation times), you allow your members to schedule vacations, plan to be away, and yet still make their small group meetings a priority.

During breaks, continue to communicate with your members via email and in person. Schedule social times together. Meet for prayer. Serve together. You're not cutting off all communication. Instead, you're simply allowing for a pause from the routine. Taking breaks will undergird your longevity as a leader and keep your meetings from becoming stale.

The Lord gave us the wonderful gift of rest. I hope you'll use this gift.

# 12

# One-on-Ones

*The Meetings Outside of Your Meetings*

Tim and Jennifer met when she began working for his company. Their coworker relationship eventually grew into a casual friendship. Tim looked forward to seeing Jennifer in the break room or talking with her in the hallway. If he saw her walk past his office door, he would suddenly find a reason to take a lap around the office or make a trip to the restroom, hoping he'd "just happen" to bump into her. He enjoyed their friendly banter.

After a few months, these casual conversations turned into deeper discussions. Tim began texting and calling Jennifer outside of office hours. He appreciated the way she listened to him and the fact that they agreed on so many issues. Not once did they ever argue about anything.

Unlike his conversations with his wife.

Eventually, Tim's wife discovered his text exchanges with

Jennifer and saw the call log on his phone. She confronted Tim and accused him of having an affair. He denied it, but he also told her he wanted a divorce. He was tired of their constant fighting and needed a change. He longed for a different life, one that didn't involve her. Tim left home and moved in with a friend.

Tim's wife contacted their small group leader and his wife. She wept bitterly as she recounted her conversation with Tim. This couple dropped everything and drove to her house. They listened, offered a few words of counsel, and spent most of their remaining time praying for her and Tim.

Then the group leader contacted Tim. With persistence, he insisted that Tim come to his home, and there he lovingly confronted Tim about his decision to leave his wife and kids. Tim evaded, excused, and minimized, but the leader continued to push him toward biblical truth. Tim left that evening without committing to anything; however, the small group leader didn't give up. He called and texted Tim virtually every day. A week later, Tim returned home and reconciled with his wife. They went to counseling, and today their marriage is healthier than it's ever been.

Although the names have been changed to protect the couple's privacy, this is a very real story of a marriage that was saved through the ministry of a small group leader. He had the opportunity to speak truth into Tim's life because they had connected outside of their small group meetings. Their bond made it difficult for Tim to ignore the repeated requests to meet. The leader also continued to pray and speak truth into Tim's life. His persistence changed the trajectory of Tim's life and the lives of his wife and children.

A necessary component of shepherding your small group involves interacting with members outside of your scheduled meetings. You and your spouse can meet one-on-one with members of the same gender, or all together as couples. As you build these relationships, you will gain the ability to speak truth into the lives of your group members. In Tim's case, the time the small group leader invested in him outside of those meetings put relationship capital in his pocket, which he quickly spent when Tim's better judgment became clouded.

Moreover, these additional one-on-one or two-on-two meetings will allow you to go deeper in your discussions. You can ask more specific, individualized questions. You'll discover ways to shepherd the members of your group with intentionality.

Meeting with group members doesn't have to consume hours of your time each week or month. It's not a full-time job. But a little extra effort on your part will make a tremendous difference in the health of your small group and the lives of your members.

Here are several ways you can minister to individuals in your group.

1. *Grab lunch or coffee.* Don't feel obligated to do this every week or even every month; however, meeting once a quarter or a couple times a year with a group member for a quick lunch or coffee will be incredibly beneficial. Use these times to listen to their stories, learn more about their lives, and have an intentional conversation about spiritual matters. Consider asking the following questions:

   • Are you growing spiritually?
   • What is your favorite spiritual discipline?
   • What are your biggest struggles right now?
   • Tell me how you came to know the Lord.
   • When have you felt closest to the Lord?
   • What is God teaching you these days?

It is rare, especially for men, to have conversations of this nature. Most people aren't accustomed to asking or answering questions about their spiritual lives. Depending on the individual and your relationship, you may need to enter the spiritual pool from the shallow end and wade in slowly. Asking "What's the biggest sin you've ever committed?" right out of the gate will probably scare them into changing churches.

Also use this time to get feedback on their small group experience. Ask for suggestions. This will not only give you ideas for how to lead better, but it will also increase the other person's investment in the group. They will be far more likely to attend, be prepared, and engage in group discussions if they feel a sense of ownership.

2. *Form a small group within your small group.* This was something Jesus practiced. He led a small group of twelve men; however, he spent more time with Peter, James, and John. He invested heavily in these three men because they would become—along with Paul—the primary leaders of the early church.

   Perhaps you could meet separately with two or three individuals in your group for a time of prayer and accountability. Several years ago, a leader in our church began meeting with two guys from his group each week for prayer. One was a brand-new believer, and the other had only recently returned to his faith. This leader shared with me that he only started meeting with these two individuals because a pastor suggested doing so during a small group training session. He wasn't sure what would happen. After several weeks of meeting, one of the men confessed to the leader that he struggled with pornography. They met together each week for accountability, and this man eventually found freedom from his addiction.

These "inner circle" meetings may be only for a brief period, especially if you are doing a specific study together. Or you may decide to continue meeting indefinitely. It all depends on what you believe will be the most beneficial for these individuals and your group.

3. *Send texts, emails, social media messages.* Let's face it: We're all busy. We all have work, family, and social commitments. Everyone has a lot on their plate. You may lead a group of couples with children, and they are overwhelmed. Evenings are consumed with sporting events, homework, and social activities. It's challenging to stay connected.

One easy way is through text, emails, group chat apps, social media, or whatever the latest digital connection platform happens to be. For example—perhaps when your group is on a break—you can do a weekly devotion and send comments through social media. Maybe you can commit to read through a book of the Bible together, and you can send weekly reminders about the chapters to read that week.

Again, this doesn't have to consume hours of your time. When necessary, you can take a break from doing these "extra" tasks or ask someone in the group to assist. Train other leaders by encouraging them to reach out and schedule individual meetings.

4. *Plan time for fellowship.* Every conversation and interaction doesn't have to be deep and spiritual. There is value

in eating, laughing, and playing together. Schedule times to have fun.

As you plan get-togethers outside of your scheduled group meetings, consider the following guidelines:

- *Don't meet one-on-one with members of the opposite sex.* Protect yourself and your group by keeping good boundaries in your relationships. If you're married, avoid potential criticism, emotional entanglements, and temptation by not meeting individually with a member of the opposite sex. An inappropriate relationship within your small group will destroy the health of your marriage, your group, and potentially your entire church. Don't buy into the lie, "Oh, that would never happen." There are countless terrible stories where it happened in the lives of those who never thought it would.
- *Call for backup.* Perhaps as group members open up to you, you realize they need counseling that is beyond your skill set. Or maybe someone confesses something that may have legal ramifications. Do not hesitate to contact a pastor or counselor in your church for help if you are in over your head.

  If someone ever says, "I'll tell you something, but you have to promise me you'll never tell anyone," do not make that promise. You can say, "I will keep what you say confidential—*unless* what you tell me is that you've hurt someone or are about to hurt yourself or someone else. Then I cannot remain silent." If the person does share this type information with you, you will likely have an ethical responsibility to report the information to a pastor, another church leader, or authorities outside of the church.

- *Don't waste opportunities.* Not every conversation needs to be spiritually heavy. But do you really want a member of your small group going an entire year without someone asking, "How is your relationship with God?" Your group members need to be challenged. These intentional conversations will be invaluable in their faith journey.

Appointments outside of your scheduled meetings can bear significant fruit in your ministry as a small group leader. Again, leading a small group is an art, not a science. As you gauge the spiritual vitality of your members, you'll be able to determine the best ways to minister to them, both individually and as a group.

# 13

# Necessary Endings

*When Your Group Needs to Dissolve*

SMALL GROUPS AREN'T meant to last forever. Though some may meet for twenty or more years, others will meet for only a season or two. Perhaps you know of groups that have lasted for several decades. However, longevity isn't always good and healthy for a small group. There are numerous reasons for the life cycle of a group to reach its necessary ending. Some are intentional and natural. Some will be difficult and awkward. Others have to do with you as the leader.

## Good Endings

Here are several positive reasons for a small group to disband.

1. *An intentional plan exists to divide and reach more people.*
   Multiplication could be the plan from the beginning or a
   decision made later in the life of the group. For example,

if your church is growing exponentially and there is a dire need for new groups, a pastor or other leader may ask your group to plant another group in order to accommodate these new church attenders.

We see this very thing happening in the early church:

> The Lord added to their number daily those who were being saved.
>
> ACTS 2:47

> In those days when the number of disciples was increasing . . .
>
> ACTS 6:1

> The word of God spread. The number of disciples in Jerusalem increased rapidly, and a large number of priests became obedient to the faith.
>
> ACTS 6:7

The church in Jerusalem expanded quickly, necessitating the fast-track development of leaders to disciple the new converts. In a season of rapid growth, the small group ministry may be forced to take an all-hands-on-deck approach. Members with group experience are conscripted into serving as leaders to handle the influx of new individuals. If this happens in your church, enjoy the Lord's blessing and encourage others to help accommodate that growth.

2. *The group ends to scatter into new groups.* In my church, as I mentioned in chapter 11, we operate on the semester system. We essentially start and restart each semester to

give our members an opportunity to gracefully exit their small group if needed. For example, members may want to switch to a small group that is studying a particular topic. Or their life circumstances may have changed, and they need a group that meets at a different time. If enough members want a change, the group may choose to dissolve and go their separate ways.

3. *The group ends due to changes in group dynamics.* This often happens as members move into different life stages. For example, a small group of young singles may meet for a year or two and then dissolve when several members get married. A young couples group may realize the group needs to dissolve when couples start having children and their needs and schedules begin to shift. Sometimes, group members will decide to move from a homogeneous group to one that is more diverse—for example, from a young couples group to one with a range of ages and stages of life.

All of these reasons are intentional, reasonable, and organic endings for a small group. More than likely, there won't be a need for difficult or awkward conversations. Members will go their separate ways and remain friends. After the small group ends, they will happily serve together on a committee or in a ministry at the church. They will recall with fondness the time they spent together in a small group. They will see each other in the hallway at church and speak, hug, and make plans to get together for lunch.

## Forced Endings

Sometimes a small group will come to an uncomfortable, forced ending. This typically happens when the leader realizes that the group is no longer serving its intended purpose. Members aren't living out Proverbs 27:17: "As iron sharpens iron, so one person sharpens another." Individuals are walking away from meetings just as spiritually dull as when they entered.

When a leader decides to dissolve a group, it may come as a surprise to some of the members who thought everything was going quite well. Though necessary, forced endings can often be awkward and difficult, and they may have repercussions in the church.

Here are some reasons that a group may be compelled to dissolve.

1. *Overfamiliarity.* When a small group becomes engrained to the point that members no longer challenge one another, it may be time to dissolve the group and shake things up. One sign of a group that has become overfamiliar is when they start to excuse one another's sin by saying, "Oh, he's just that way. That's just Bill being Bill." Though these group members may be close and care about one another, they've lost the capacity to foster spiritual growth.

2. *Stagnation.* When a group isn't growing spiritually—and maybe their numbers have decreased as well—it's probably time to dissolve the group. If some members have moved or passed away and no one has been added to the group, it's often a good thing for everyone to move on to a different group that has more vitality.

3. *Conflict.* Maybe a couple in the group has gone through a nasty divorce, or two members have a severe conflict. Perhaps an individual has been arrested or accused of misconduct. Sometimes the right answer is to stay together and weather the storm; but when dramatic events completely

change the dynamics of the group, it may be time for a fresh start.

4. *Unhealthy group dynamics.* As we saw in chapter 2, sometimes small groups are unhealthy. Maybe they've become a therapeutic group or a social group; or they're no longer focused on God's Word and growing in their faith. If an unhealthy small group cannot be moved toward a healthier dynamic, it's probably best to dissolve the group to allow members to find a more suitable situation.

5. *Disruption.* We've looked at how a difficult member can disrupt a small group. If the group leader and/or other members have confronted this individual and made repeated attempts to address the behavior, but to no avail, the only path forward is to end the group.

6. *Burnout.* Finally, a small group may need to end because of the leader. Perhaps you need a break and there is no one to take your place. Though I hope you will serve for many years as a small group leader, there are occasions when your wisest move is to step aside. Here are a few questions to consider before you make a decision.

- Does the Lord want me to do something else for a season?
- Do I dread my small group meetings?
- Do I need a break for my own spiritual and mental health?
- Is there a significant sin issue in my life that is hindering my walk with the Lord and my ability to shepherd group members?

- Is there a reason I'm unable to support the leadership of the church?

If you answered *yes* to any of the above questions, you might want to talk with a trusted friend or a pastor in the church about your concerns. If you ultimately decide to step down, please give your pastor or the leader of your small group ministry plenty of notice and help them think through the next steps for your group.

Necessary endings aren't always easy. However, for the good of your members and the church, they are sometimes the best option.

# 14

# Press On

*A Final Word of Encouragement*

I HAVE A FRIEND who started a men's small group. He wanted to make a difference where he lived and ultimately to have an influence that spread beyond his community. He understood very well the mission to go and make disciples. He had a great passion for life-on-life discipleship and for others to discover the great joy of an intimate relationship with God.

This guy is a dreamer, and he had a big vision. He developed a plan to pour himself into several men for some time, eventually releasing them to go and do the same thing with others. His one small group, he hoped, would lead to the formation of many more small groups. In his mind, he saw some of these men teaming up with their wives to lead couples groups. He envisioned women from those groups intentionally discipling other women. With everything in him, he believed that choosing the *right men* and guiding them in the *right way* would ignite a process of discipleship that would have a significant impact on his community.

He spent hours praying for the Lord to direct him to the men he should ask to join his small group. After a lot of praying, thinking, and observing the lives of men around him, he asked several to join him. My friend intentionally kept them in the dark about his long-range goals. If he said, "And one day I want you to lead a small group much like this one," they might not agree to join him. *One step at a time*, he thought. *Eventually, they will be ready to lead others in discipleship.*

His group met often. They studied the Scriptures. They prayed together. They ate together. They even took trips together. My friend was determined to disciple these men through his example as well as his teaching. He gave as much time as he could to immersing himself in their lives. He asked them the tough questions. He challenged them. He taught them. He prayed for them. He served them. He invested hours in each of these men.

As a result, these men grew in their faith. Slowly, over time, they became devoted to God. They began living differently, with a determination to follow God wholeheartedly.

Mostly.

At several points, things didn't go as planned. There was one instance when a couple of the guys maneuvered for a privileged opportunity. When the others got wind of their scheme, they became jealous. Their actions divided the group, and the leader had to do some quick damage control.

There were other times when my friend spent a lot of time teaching certain truths, only to see one or more of the men fail miserably. Some of his guys would demonstrate an incredible trust in the Lord, then later exhibit no faith at all. Those times broke my friend's heart. He desperately wanted these men to get it, yet they struggled to trust in and follow the Lord fully.

There was one particularly low point in the life of this small group. One of the members fell into egregious sin. His choices reflected the fact that he had not really been committed to the other men or to his walk with the Lord. Perhaps it was simply the fellowship that drew him to join this small group. Some suspected he had joined the group because•he believed it would help him succeed in business. Others claimed that he became disillusioned with the leader, that he thought my friend made several bad decisions regarding the group's direction.

Whatever the reason, this man's actions devastated the others. He was forced to leave the small group. His sin and his exit from their lives changed the group dynamics. For some time, these men quit meeting. Some wondered if the group had dissolved forever.

My friend was heartbroken. It was the lowest point in his life. It looked as if he'd failed in his mission. He had spent years investing in these men—for nothing. His dream was dead.

You've undoubtedly heard of my friend. In fact, I'm guessing you know him and also count him as a friend. Moreover, you've likely read the stories of how his small group struggled. Those who were eyewitnesses of these events reported them happening like this:

James and John, the sons of Zebedee, came to him.
"Teacher," they said, "we want you to do for us whatever we ask."
"What do you want me to do for you?" he asked.
They replied, "Let one of us sit at your right and the other at your left in your glory." . . .

When the ten heard about this, they became
indignant with James and John.

MARK 10:35-37, 41

"Lord, if it's you," Peter replied, "tell me to come to you
on the water."

"Come," he said.

Then Peter got down out of the boat, walked on the
water and came toward Jesus. But when he saw the wind,
he was afraid and, beginning to sink, cried out, "Lord,
save me!"

Immediately Jesus reached out his hand and caught
him. "You of little faith," he said, "why did you doubt?"

MATTHEW 14:28-31

Judas went to the chief priests and the officers of the
temple guard and discussed with them how he might
betray Jesus. They were delighted and agreed to give him
money. He consented, and watched for an opportunity to
hand Jesus over to them when no crowd was present.

LUKE 22:4-6

Of course, you know the end of the story as well. Although
this small group scattered for a while, they ultimately reunited
and began living out the vision Jesus had for them. They became
leaders of other small groups. Out of those small groups, other
leaders emerged and started their own small groups. This process
continued to spread so that two thousand years later, there have
been millions of leaders discipling billions of others within the
environment of a small group.

And it all goes back to that first small group, one that experienced a lot of problems.

In the history of Christianity, there has been only one perfect small group leader. You just read about him. Even though he was sinless, completely righteous, and the greatest teacher and leader who ever walked the earth, his group still had problems.

If the perfect leader had issues in his group, should we expect anything different?

There is no perfect small group. Group members will disappoint you. You'll spend hours preparing for a meeting, and they'll send you a text thirty minutes beforehand informing you that they can't come because of an offer to go to the movies with some friends.

Or they won't text you at all. Instead, they just won't show up, and when asked later about their absence, they will simply say, "Something came up."

You'll pour your life into discipling a new Christian only to see him or her head right back into a life of sin.

A couple in your small group will call to let you know that they're divorcing.

Someone will try to take your group in the wrong direction. They will be mad at you for something you said. Or did. Or didn't say or do.

They will gossip. They will act selfishly. They will drop out of the group without any explanation.

In hundreds of other ways, members may disappoint you.

Here's my advice: Press on. Keep going. Continue to lead. Address difficult situations, but don't give up. Jesus faced disappointments with his small group. In his humanity, I'm sure he had thoughts of giving up on these men. At times, perhaps, he regretted saying to them, "Come and follow me."

However, even in their struggles, God had a great plan for this small group.

He does for yours as well.

God has called you to disciple your small group. As you are faithful in serving him and your members, he will give you more victories than defeats. He will allow you to see lives changed, relationships healed, prayers answered, faith ignited and deepened, and so much more.

So press on, my friend. Press on.

# About the Author

Kevin Mills is lead pastor of Northway Church in Macon, Georgia. He is a graduate of Mercer University and Samford University, with a master's degree in theology. He and his wife, Katie, have four children.

If you liked this book, you'll want to get involved in

# Church Member Equip!

— — —

Do you have a desire to learn more about serving God through your local church?

Would you like to see how God can use you in new and exciting ways?

Get your church involved in Church Member Equip, an online ministry designed to prepare church leaders and church members to better serve God's mission and purpose.

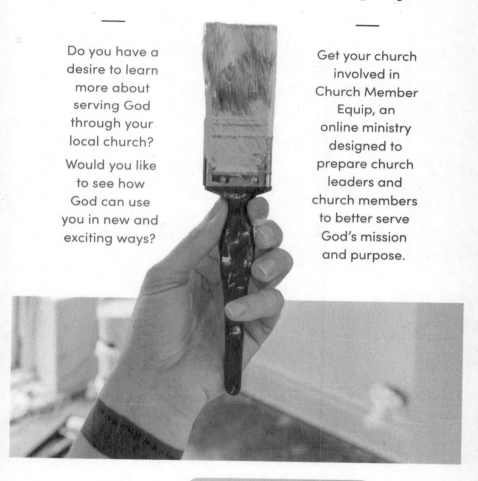

Check us out at    **www.ChurchMemberEquip.com**

**CHURCH ANSWERS**
FEATURING THOM RAINER

CP1749